Introduction to the Accounting Process

Introduction to the Accounting Process

C.A.M. Klerks-van de Nouland

H.J.M. van Sten-Van 't Hoff

A. Tressel

First edition

Noordhoff Uitgevers Groningen | Houten

Cover design: G2K Designers
Cover illustration: Photodisc

If you have any comments or queries about this or any other publication, please contact: Noordhoff Uitgevers bv, Afdeling Hoger Onderwijs, Antwoordnummer 13, 9700 VB Groningen, e-mail: info@noordhoff.nl

0 1 2 3 4 5 / 14 13 12 11 10

© 2010 Noordhoff Uitgevers bv Groningen/Houten, the Netherlands

Apart from the exceptions provided by or pursuant to the Copyright Act of 1912, no part of this publication may be reproduced, stored in an automated retrieval system or transmitted, in any form or by any means, electronic, mechanical, photocopying, recording or otherwise, without the prior written approval of the publisher. Insofar as the making of reprographic copies from this publication is permitted on the basis of Article 16h of the Copyright Act of 1912, the compensation owed must be provided to the Stichting Reprorecht (postbus 3060, 2130 KB Hoofddorp, Netherlands, www.cedar.nl/reprorecht). To use specific sections of this publication for anthologies, readers or other compilations (Article 16 of the Copyright Act of 1912), contact the Stichting PRO (Stichting Publicatie- en Reproductierechten Organisatie, postbus 3060, 2130 KB Hoofddorp, Netherlands, www.cedar.nl/pro).

All rights reserved. No part of this publication may be reproduced, stored in a retrieval system, or transmitted, in any form or by any means, electronic, mechanical, photocopying, recording or otherwise without the prior written permission of the publisher.

ISBN 978-90-01-78923-7
NUR 786

Preface

This is the first English edition of the Dutch version of *Introduction to the Accounting Process*. This edition incorporates certain changes. This edition includes three new chapters (Part III, International aspects of accounting, chapters 14, 15 and 16). The major change is the internet site that has been added to the book. Part of this site is accessible to students and another is for teachers only. The students' part includes sheets on which to answer problems/do exercises, as well as the solutions to some of these. Solutions to other problems are accessible to teachers only.

The new internet site also includes a case study that can be used by teachers and students to practise both manual and automated accounting.

The number of exercises has been adjusted in such a way that they reflect what happens in businesses.

The text contains references to other chapters so that the student can easily find related information. Key words in the margin help students to navigate their way through the book; these are included in the index at the end of the book.

The course consists of four parts:

Part I: The book-keeping system. In this part students will learn step by step how to record financial facts in the book-keeping system.

Part II: Special accounting entries. Attention will be paid to a number of frequently occurring issues.

Part III: International aspects of accounting, focusing on different formats for financial statements, ratio analysis and cash flow statements.

Part IV: A case study. By working on this, students can judge whether they have mastered what they learned on this course.

All chapters include examples and a number of exercises, which aid students to assess their level of understanding.

Apart from the above-mentioned improvements, a new layout helps guide students through the book.

This introductory course is suited for students in universities and business schools who lack basic knowledge of the accounting process.

Table of contents

Introduction *9*

Part I
The accounting system *11*

1. Balance sheet *12*
2. Ledger accounts *17*
3. Eight-column financial statements *25*
4. Closing the ledger accounts *33*
5. Journal entries *38*
6. Special journals *46*
7. Sub-ledger accounts *58*

Part II
Special entries *75*

8. The decimal accounting system *76*
9. VAT (value-added tax) *79*
10. Withdrawals *88*
11. Sales revenues *95*
12. Various entries in cash books *100*
13. Adjusting entries *106*

Part III
International aspects of accounting *111*

14. Various formats of financial statements *112*
15. Ratio analysis *119*
16. Cash flow statements *129*

Part IV

17. Case study: Hoovers *141*

Index *151*

Introduction

'Anybody who runs a business is obliged to record his capital and all that concerns his business in such a way that rights and duties can be derived from these records.'

This article in the Commercial Code is still valid. It means that in any business all events influencing assets, receivables or liabilities must be recorded. In the past this happened in a number of 'books', hence book-keeping. Nowadays, the word 'accounting' is applied, though this is more than merely registering financial facts.
Financial accounting is aimed at providing financial information to external stakeholders, such as shareholders and banks. Investors can assess how management has performed its tasks (accountability) and can use the financial information as a basis for future investment decisions, though they should realise that financial statements always relate to previous years.
Another major change, in the final quarter of the last century, was the introduction of the computer. There is hardly any business in which the administration is not automated. Most (mostly small) businesses that do not perform the recording themselves outsource this activity to specialised accounting firms, which apply one of the many computerised accounting programs.
Using a computer does not help anyone understand the accounting process. After making the necessary entries, the computer runs several invisible procedures, and pressing one button will show a new balance sheet and income statement.
The only way to understand book-keeping is to do it manually, preferably with pencil and eraser. After this, it is not hard to switch to automated accounting, realising that the computerised process is identical to the manual one.
In this introductory course students familiarise themselves with the accounting process and the way in which financial facts are recorded manually.

The course consists of four parts. In Part I, the basics of the accounting process are outlined by constructing the accounting system. Part II discusses some common problems, such as VAT, withdrawals and adjustments. Part III focuses on international aspects of accounting. In Part IV, all topics in the course are integrated in a case study. By working on this, students can assess their level of understanding.
The full course is based on the administration of a firm with the legal form of sole proprietor. Later in their studies students will realise that different enterprises with different legal forms will apply the same accounting systems, only with more accounts.
Within the scope of this book, no attention will be paid to internal control, though this does not mean that it is unimportant.

An internet site is linked to this book. The site consists of a part for students and a part for teachers only. Students can find sheets on which to answer problems/do exercises, as well as solutions to some of these. Teachers have access to the solutions of all the other problems. The site also includes a case study, Plug and Play, with three months of financial facts. The case study can also be used in a computerised accounting course.

Since not all teaching institutions use the same accounting program, financial facts for Plug and Play's first month of existence are available on the teachers' part of the site. This enables teachers to prepare the basis of the accounting scheme, which students can use to continue with the facts for the following three months.

This introductory course is meant for students in universities and business schools who lack the basics of accounting.

After successfully finishing this course students will be able to:
- record simple financial facts in journals and sub-ledgers
- prepare journal entries and record them in the ledger system
- prepare the trial balance
- apply the decimal accounting system
- understand the accounting process.

In this book we use American terms for specific accounting concepts. The following list shows the equivalent terms in American and British usage:

American term	**English term**
cash	bank, petty cash
accounts receivable	debtors
accounts payable	creditors
inventories	stock
note payable	bank loan
net income	profit

Part I The accounting system

A balance sheet shows assets and liabilities. Each firm prepares a balance sheet once a year to show stakeholders the firm's financial position. After the balance sheet has been prepared, subsequent financial facts will mean it has to be changed.
This part of the book will show how financial facts will be recorded in order to prepare a new balance sheet at the end of the year. This balance sheet will then show the starting position for the following accounting year.

The following chapters are included in this part:
chapter 1   Balance sheet
chapter 2   Ledger accounts
chapter 3   Eight-column financial statements
chapter 4   Closing the ledger accounts
chapter 5   Journal entries
chapter 6   Special journals
chapter 7   Sub-ledger accounts

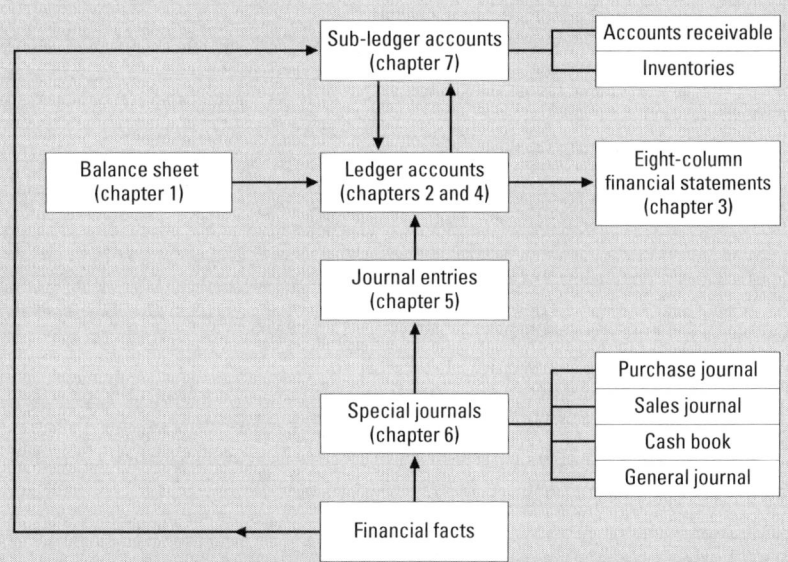

Balance sheet

Balance sheet

Each accounting process starts with a balance sheet.
A balance sheet shows assets and liabilities at a certain moment. The real values of these assets and liabilities can be determined by listing what the firm possesses.

Assets
Liabilities
Credit side

Assets are mentioned on the debit side of the balance sheet (left), liabilities or debt on the credit side (right).

Figure 1.1

Debit	Balance sheet 1 January (in €)		Credit
Inventories	20,000	Equity	25,000
Accounts receivable	13,000	Accounts payable	14,000
Cash	6,000		
	39,000		39,000

Accounts receivable

Accounts payable

Equity

Additional information:
Accounts receivable are customers who purchased goods on account; the number on the balance sheet shows the total receivable from these customers.
Accounts payable are suppliers from whom the firm purchased goods on account; the amount shows the total payable to these suppliers.
Equity: this is a special sort of liability; it is the amount the owner of the firm would receive if the company were to be liquidated. Assets will then be sold, debt will be paid and the remainder is for the owner. If the real values of assets and liabilities equal the amounts on the balance sheet, the remainder equals equity. However, it is not a debt in the real sense of the word. If the firm's administration is separate from the owner's private administration, then it is easy to consider equity as the firm's debt to the owner. (This is known as the 'business theory'.)
A balance sheet needs to balance, which means the debit total needs to equal the credit total.
A balance sheet shows the firm's financial position at one moment. Each time something happens that may influence one or more items on the balance sheet, a new balance sheet will develop. The effect of financial facts on the balance sheet is as follows:

Figure 1.2

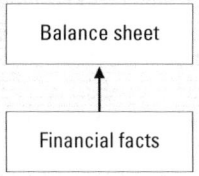

Example 1.1

3 January   Purchased on account products with a value of €5,000.

The 'inventories' account will increase by €5,000 and the 'accounts payable' account by €5,000 as well. The new balance sheet is as follows:

Figure 1.3

Debit	Balance sheet 3 January (in €)		Credit
Inventories	25,000	Equity	25,000
Accounts receivable	13,000	Accounts payable	19,000
Cash	6,000		
	44,000		44,000

Both debit and credit sides increase by €5,000; the balance sheet stays in balance.

Example 1.2

4 January   Paid cash to a supplier: €3,000.

The 'cash' account will decrease by €3,000 and the 'accounts payable' account will decrease by €3,000 as well.

Figure 1.4

Debit	Balance sheet 4 January (in €)		Credit
Inventories	25,000	Equity	25,000
Accounts receivable	13,000	Accounts payable	16,000
Cash	3,000		
	41,000		41,000

The equilibrium remains here as well: both sides of the balance sheet decrease by the same amount.

■ **Example 1.3**

5 January   Sold products on account for €6,000. These products had a purchase price of €4,000.

The 'accounts receivable' account will increase by €6,000; the 'inventories' account will decrease by €4,000. The difference between the sales price and the purchase price is the gross profit.
The owner is entitled to receive this gross profit; the company's 'debt' to the owner increases, and that is why the 'equity' account increases by €2,000.

Figure 1.5

Debit	Balance sheet 5 January (in €)		Credit
Inventories	21,000	Equity	27,000
Accounts receivable	19,000	Accounts payable	16,000
Cash	3,000		
	43,000		43,000

The debit side of the balance sheet shows two changes, the credit side just one. After these changes the balance sheet is again in equilibrium. ■

■ **Example 1.4**

6 January   Paid advertising expenses in cash, €500.

The 'cash' account decreases by €500. Advertising expenses are costs that reduce profit, and thus reduce the owner's equity by €500.

Figure 1.6

Debit	Balance sheet 6 January (in €)		Credit
Inventories	21,000	Equity	26,500
Accounts receivable	19,000	Accounts payable	16,000
Cash	2,500		
	42,500		42,500

Again, after the changes the balance sheet balances. ■

Exercises

1.1 a The following balance sheet will be affected by the financial facts mentioned below. Indicate the changes.

Figure 1.7

Debit		Balance sheet 1 January (in €)		Credit
Equipment	13,000	Equity		37,000
Inventories	27,000	Loan		15,000
Accounts receivable	33,000	Accounts payable		23,000
Cash	2,000			
	75,000			75,000

10 January Purchased on account equipment with a value of €3,500.
16 January Products sold for €1,500, cash received. The purchase price of these products was €1,000.
21 January Paid back €1,000 on the loan.
25 January Paid maintenance costs, €500, in cash.

b Prepare the balance sheet at 25 January.

1.2 S. Klaver Company is a retailer of open fireplaces.
On 2 January 2009 it was discovered that some of the assets and liabilities listed below belong to the firm's capital. If relevant, the amounts are based on the fair value at 2 January 2009.
Prepare Klaver's balance sheet at 2 January 2009.
- A computer with hardware, value €1,700.
- 3 fireplaces, type Warinda, total purchase price €3,600.
- 2 fireplaces, type Kolos, total purchase price €1,600.
- 4 fireplaces, type Sindor, total purchase price €6,000.
- The bank statement at 31 December 2008 shows a debit balance of €3,200.
- Outstanding receivable, J. Havelaar: €1,900 for delivering a fireplace.
- A filing cabinet, value €800.
- 1 desk with chair, value €2,700.
- 20 Unilever shares, market value per share on 2 January: €30.
- Still owing to supplier Van Houten LLC: €6,300 for delivering fireplaces.
- Still to pay: VAT €1,230.
- A document showing that the firm owes €10,000 to H. Verhoef.
- In cash, €150.

1.3 At 1 July 2009 a wholesaler in office equipment has prepared the following balance sheet (in €):

Figure 1.8

Debit	Balance sheet 1 July 2009		Credit
Equipment	17,400	Equity	39,820
Marketable securities	8,000	Loan	16,000
Inventories	27,520	Accounts payable	21,900
Accounts receivable	28,200	Bank loan	3,300
Cash	300	Expenses payable	400
	81,420		81,420

The inventories consist of 24 desks at €900 each and 16 chairs at €370 each.

The following financial facts relate to July 2009:

03/07 An amount of €300 was withdrawn from the bank and deposited in office cash.
08/07 Paid the expenses payable in cash, €400. This was for maintenance work, carried out in June: not paid until now, and an invoice has not been received.
10/07 Purchased 3 desks at €900 each and 5 chairs at €370 each.
14/07 Sold 1,000 shares and received €5,000 in cash. The shares were purchased for €4,500.
15/07 Paid in cash the invoice for telephone expenses, €300.
20/07 Sold on account 4 desks at €1,200 each and 3 chairs at €500 each. Furniture and invoice have been sent today.
21/07 Collected from the warehouse 1 desk and 1 chair for use in own office.
24/07 Paid a supplier €2,800 in cash and received cash from a customer, €7,620. The bank has credited our account with €4,820.
28/07 Collected from the warehouse 1 desk and 1 chair, to be used by eldest daughter in her study.
31/07 Paid €1,150 in cash for the semi-annual redemption of the loan, €1,000, and €150 interest for this period.
31/07 Depreciation on equipment for the month of July, €200.

Indicate (by date) which accounts will change and prepare the balance sheet as at 31 July 2009.

Ledger accounts

After preparing the balance sheet in the last exercise of chapter 1, it should be clear to you that preparing a new balance sheet after each financial fact is complicated. A small firm has 20 or 30 accounts on its balance sheet and the number of invoices, cash receipts, etc. is obviously much larger than in the exercises. Think of a firm like Philips or Unilever!

The solution to this problem is preparing the ledger.

Ledger

The term 'ledger' dates from the time that accounting was done manually on cards (see Preface). These cards, which together form the ledger, are called 'accounts'.

Accounts

For each item on the balance sheet, an account will be opened. The balance of the account will be recorded as debit or credit on the relevant account, depending whether the account is shown as debit or credit on the balance sheet.

Chapter 1 showed the following balance sheet:

Figure 2.1

Debit	Balance sheet 1 January (in €)		Credit
Inventories	20,000	Equity	25,000
Accounts receivable	13,000	Accounts payable	14,000
Cash	6,000		
	39,000		39,000

The ledger is as follows:

Figure 2.2

Debit			Inventories (in €)			Credit
Date	Description	Amount	Date	Description		Amount
01/01	Balance	20,000				

Figure 2.3

Debit			Accounts receivable (in €)			Credit
Date	Description	Amount	Date	Description		Amount
01/01	Balance	13,000				

Figure 2.4

Debit			Cash (in €)			Credit
Date	Description	Amount	Date	Description		Amount
01/01	Balance	6,000				

Figure 2.5

Debit			Equity (in €)			Credit
Date	Description	Amount	Date	Description		Amount
01/01	Balance	25,000				

Figure 2.6

Debit			Accounts payable (in €)			Credit
Date	Description	Amount	Date	Description		Amount
01/01	Balance	14,000				

If all the ledger accounts are put together, they form the original balance sheet.

Financial facts that influenced the balance directly in chapter 1 will now be recorded on the ledger accounts.

The accounting scheme looks as follows:

Figure 2.7

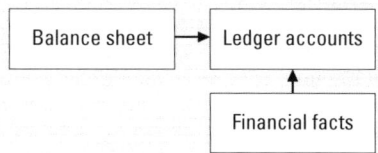

Example 2.1

3 January   Purchased on account products with a value of €5,000.

The balance sheet 'inventories' account increases with €5,000. This will be recorded as a debit on the 'inventories' account.

> Accounting rule 1   **An increase in assets is recorded on the debit side of an asset account.**

Figure 2.8

Debit			Inventories (in €)				Credit
Date	Description		Amount	Date	Description		Amount
01/01	Balance		20,000				
03/01	Purchased on account		5,000				

The balance sheet 'accounts payable' account will increase as well. This will be recorded on the credit side of the 'accounts payable' ledger account.

> Accounting rule 2   **An increase in a liability (debt) is credited to a liability account.**

Figure 2.9

Debit			Accounts payable (in €)				Credit
Date	Description		Amount	Date	Description		Amount
				01/01	Balance		14,000
				03/01	Inventories		5,000

Remark
At this stage it is sometimes hard to decide on the description. However, accounting is an information system, so always use a description that provides information. After discussing the full accounting cycle, it will be clear what description you should insert.

Example 2.2

4 January   Paid cash to a supplier, €3,000.

The balance sheet 'cash' account will decrease by €3,000. We could indicate this with a minus sign on the debit side of the 'cash' ledger account. However, minus signs are never used in accounting (with one exception, outlined in chapter 6). Instead, we record the amount on the credit side. By deducting the amount on the credit side from the amount on the debit side, we find the actual amount of cash.

> Accounting rule 3   **A decrease in an asset is credited to the asset account.**

Figure 2.10

Debit			Cash (in €)			Credit
Date	Description	Amount		Date	Description	Amount
01/01	Balance	6,000		04/01	Accounts payable	3,000

The balance sheet 'accounts payable' account decreases by €3,000; here also, a minus sign on the credit side will not be used: the amount will be recorded on the other side. By deducting the debit amount from the credit amount, the correct total of outstanding liabilities is found.

> Accounting rule 4   **A decrease in a liability/debt is debited to a liability account.**

Figure 2.11

Debit			Accounts payable (in €)			Credit
Date	Description	Amount		Date	Description	Amount
04/01	Cash	3,000		01/01	Balance	14,000
				03/01	Inventories	5,000

Example 2.3

5 January   Sold on account products with a sales price of €6,000. The purchase price amounted to €4,000.

The balance sheet 'accounts receivable' account increases; we apply accounting rule 1.

Figure 2.12

Debit		**Accounts receivable** (in €)					Credit
Date	Description		Amount	Date	Description		Amount
01/01	Balance		13,000				
05/01	Products		6,000				

The balance sheet 'inventories' account decreases; we apply accounting rule 3.

Figure 2.13

Debit		**Inventories** (in €)					Credit
Date	Description		Amount	Date	Description		Amount
01/01	Balance		20,000	05/01	Sold on account		4,000
03/01	Purchased on account		5,000				

Specialised equity accounts

The profit, €2,000, increases the firm's 'debt' to the owner and thus increases equity. The amount should thus be credited to the 'equity' ledger account (accounting rule 2). However, the 'equity' account is never debited or credited throughout the year. Instead, specialised equity accounts are used, showing how profit or loss is generated (revenues and expenses), resulting in a change in equity. One can use as many specialised equity accounts as one wishes. In this case, the new ledger account is called 'gross profit'.

Chapter 3 will outline how the specialised accounts will be integrated into equity.

Accounting rule 5   **An increase in equity is credited to a specialised equity account.**

Figure 2.14

Debit			Gross profit (in €)			Credit
Date	Description	Amount	Date	Description		Amount
05/01	Sales	2,000				

Example 2.4

6 January   Paid cash €500 for advertising expenses.

The balance sheet 'cash' account decreases; we apply accounting rule 3.

Figure 2.15

Debit			Cash (in €)		Credit
Date	Description	Amount	Date	Description	Amount
01/01	Balance	6,000	04/01	Accounts payable	3,000
			06/01	Advertising expenses	500

Expenses reduce gross profit, and thus equity. Here also, a specialised 'advertising expenses' account is created.

> Accounting rule 6   **A decrease in equity is debited to a specialised equity account.**

Figure 2.16

Debit			Advertising expenses (in €)		Credit
Date	Description	Amount	Date	Description	Amount
06/01	Cash	500			

Summarising the six accounting rules:
Accounting rule 1: an increase in assets is debited to an asset account.
Accounting rule 2: an increase in liability/debt is credited to a liability/debt account.
Accounting rule 3: a decrease in assets is credited to an asset account.
Accounting rule 4: a decrease in liability/debt is debited to a liability/debt account.
Accounting rule 5: an increase in equity is credited to a specialised equity account.
Accounting rule 6: a decrease in equity is debited to a specialised equity account.

Remarks:
- For all financial facts there is written evidence, such as purchase receipts, sales invoices, cash receipts, etc. For internal financial facts, such as depreciation, internal documents will be written.
- Each financial transaction is debited and credited for the same total amount, resulting in equilibrium in the ledger: the total debit amounts of all the accounts equal the total credit amounts.
- Specialised equity accounts will be created for various expenses, such as labour costs, maintenance costs, rent, etc. These show clearly what sort of expenses have been made. The 'various expenses' account will only be used incidentally.
- In the case of new assets or new liabilities (e.g. a new loan), a new ledger account with a matching name will be created (in this case 'loan').

Exercises

Answer sheet **2.1** Using the data in exercise 1.3, prepare the ledger. Create names for the specialised equity accounts. Add all the balances of the specialised equity accounts and the account 'equity' and compare the total with the equity on the balance sheet in exercise 1.3.

Answer sheet **2.2** Mr. H. Willemse is a wholesaler of baking materials.
The firm's balance sheet as at 1 January 2009 is as follows:

Figure 2.17

Debit	Balance sheet 1 January 2009 (in €)		Credit
Buildings	100,000	Equity	82,000
Equipment	20,000	Mortgage	85,000
Inventories	25,000	Accounts payable	10,000
Accounts receivable	12,000		
Cash	20,000		
	177,000		177,000

The following events took place in January 2009:

Jan. 03	Purchased on account baking materials for €6,000. Both goods and invoices have been received.
Jan. 05	Took out a loan of €20,000; cash received.
Jan. 08	Sold products for €9,000 cash; the purchase price was €5,000. Products have been dispatched.
Jan. 09	Paid a supplier €8,000.
Jan. 11	Purchased filing cabinets with a value of €7,000; paid in cash.
Jan. 14	Sold products on account for €4,000; purchase price €2500. All products have been dispatched.
Jan. 17	Paid electricity bill in cash, €600.
Jan. 18	Received cash from a customer, €1,000.
Jan. 22	Sold and delivered products for €6,000, purchase price €4,000; half of the sales have been paid for in cash; the other half will be paid for in two months.
Jan. 25	Paid cash for advertising expenses, €200.
Jan. 28	Purchased baking materials on account, €5,000. Goods have been received today.
Jan. 30	Paid wages in cash, €750.
Jan. 31	Paid cash: redemption on mortgage € 5,000
	Interest € 600
	€ 5,600

Prepare the ledger.

Eight-column financial statements

After all the financial facts have been recorded in the ledger over the whole accounting period, the balance sheet needs to be created. This can be done using the eight-column financial statements.
The scheme is as follows:

Figure 3.1

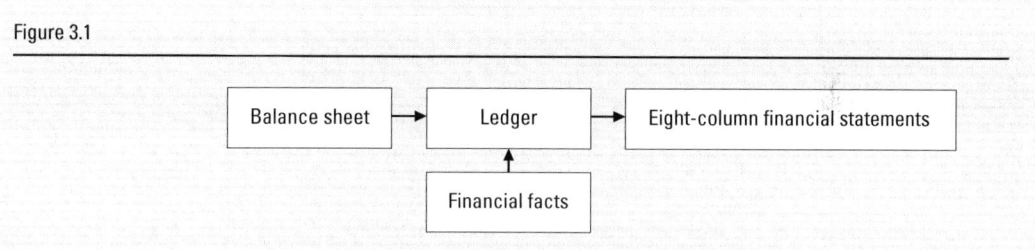

The eight-column financial statements consist of four parts, each with a debit and a credit column:
- trial balance
- balances
- income statement
- final balance sheet.

The eight-column financial statements will be prepared using the ledger accounts in chapter 2.
After all financial facts were recorded, the ledger accounts showed the following:

Figure 3.2

Debit			Inventories (in €)				Credit
Date	Description		Amount	Date	Description		Amount
01/01	Balance		20,000	05/01	Sold on account		4,000
03/01	Purchased on account		5,000				

25

Figure 3.3

Debit			Accounts receivable (in €)			Credit
Date	Description	Amount	Date	Description		Amount
01/01	Balance	13,000				
05/01	Products	6,000				

Figure 3.4

Debit			Cash (in €)		Credit
Date	Description	Amount	Date	Description	Amount
01/01	Balance	6,000	04/01	Accounts payable	3,000
			06/01	Advertising expenses	500

Figure 3.5

Debit			Equity (in €)		Credit
Date	Description	Amount	Date	Description	Amount
01/01	Balance	25,000			

Figure 3.6

Debit			Accounts payable (in €)		Credit
Date	Description	Amount	Date	Description	Amount
04/01	Cash	3,000	01/01	Balance	14,000
			03/01	Inventories	5,000

Figure 3.7

Debit			Gross profit (in €)		Credit
Date	Description	Amount	Date	Description	Amount
			05/01	Sales	2,000

Figure 3.8

Debit			Advertising expenses (in €)				Credit
Date	Description	Amount	Date	Description			Amount
06/01	Cash	500					

Trial balance

First of all, the debit and credit totals are determined for each ledger account.

In the eight-column financial statements, the names of the ledger accounts are mentioned under the heading 'accounts'. In the 'trial balance' we put the debit totals in the debit column and the credit totals in the credit column.

Leave one line open between the line with the last account and the line with the totals. This line will be needed for the income statement.

Figure 3.9

Eight-column financial statements (in €)

	Trial balance		Balances		Income statement		Final balance sheet	
Accounts	Debit	Credit	Debit	Credit	Debit	Credit	Debit	Credit
Inventories	25,000	4,000						
Accounts receivable	19,000							
Cash	6,000	3,500						
Equity		25,000						
Accounts payable	3,000	19,000						
Gross profit		2,000						
Advertising expenses	500							
	53,500	53,500						

Since the ledger is in equilibrium, the totals in the trial balance need to be equal as well.

Balances

After checking the totals on the trial balance sheet, we calculate the debit or credit balance of each ledger account and record it in the relevant column of 'balances'. Here also, debit totals needs to equal credit totals.

Figure 3.10

Eight-column financial statements (in €)

Accounts	Trial balance		Balances		Income statement		Final balance sheet	
	Debit	Credit	Debit	Credit	Debit	Credit	Debit	Credit
Inventories	25,000	4,000	21,000					
Accounts receivable	19,000		19,000					
Cash	6,000	3,500	2,500					
Equity		25,000		25,000				
Accounts payable	3,000	19,000		16,000				
Gross profit		2,000		2,000				
Advertising expenses	500		500					
	53,500	53,500	43,000	43,000				

Most figures in the 'balances', the asset and liabilities accounts, equal the figures on the new balance sheet since all the changes have been recorded through the relevant ledger accounts.

The specialised equity accounts, however, cannot be found on the balance sheet. If we had not used these specialised equity accounts, then all the relevant figures would have been recorded on the equity account. Therefore, the balance of these accounts needs to be added to equity. For this reason the balances of the specialised equity accounts are recorded in the income statement, debit balances in the debit column and credit balances in the credit column.

Income statement

The difference between the credit side (revenues) and the debit side (expenses) is net income (net loss if the debit total is higher). This figure is recorded in the open line, in the column with the lowest total. Debit and credit totals need to be equal again.

Figure 3.11

Eight-column financial statements (in €)

Accounts	Trial balance		Balances		Income statement		Final balance sheet	
	Debit	Credit	Debit	Credit	Debit	Credit	Debit	Credit
Inventories	25,000	4,000	21,000					
Accounts receivable	19,000		19,000					
Cash	6,000	3,500	2,500					
Equity		25,000		25,000				
Accounts payable	3,000	19,000		16,000				
Gross profit		2,000		2,000		2,000		
Advertising expenses	500		500		500			
Net income					1,500			
	53,500	53,500	43,000	43,000	2,000	2,000		

The owner is entitled to net income, which is why it is added to equity (a loss will be deducted from equity).

New equity will be €25,000 + €1,500 = €26,500. This figure would also be the balance of the 'equity' ledger account if we had not used the specialised equity accounts, but had recorded the financial facts directly in 'equity'. However, by using the specialised equity accounts we obtain a good overview of how profit or loss was generated.

Final balance sheet The new equity amount is recorded on the final balance sheet, together with the balances of the remaining asset and liabilities accounts. In this way all figures in the 'balances' column appear in the final balance sheet: the specialised equity accounts through the income statement and addition to equity, asset and liability accounts directly. It is clear that the final balance sheet needs to be in equilibrium.

Figure 3.12

Eight-column financial statements (in €)

Accounts	Trial balance		Balances		Income statement		Final balance sheet	
	Debit	Credit	Debit	Credit	Debit	Credit	Debit	Credit
Inventories	25,000	4,000	21,000				21,000	
Accounts receivable	19,000		19,000				19,000	
Cash	6,000	3,500	2,500				2,500	
Equity		25,000		25,000				26,500
Accounts payable	3,000	19,000		16,000				16,000
Gross profit		2,000		2,000		2,000		
Advertising expenses	500		500		500			
Net income					1,500			
	53,500	53,500	43,000	43,000	2,000	2,000	42,500	42,500

The final balance sheet in scronto form is as follows:

Figure 3.13

Debit		Balance sheet 31/1 (in €)		Credit
Inventories	21,000	Equity		26,500
Accounts receivable	19,000	Accounts payable		16,000
Cash	2,500			
	42,500			42,500

This balance sheet is exactly the same as the one at the end of chapter 1 and is the initial balance sheet for the next accounting period.

Remarks
- In the past the totals of the trial balance were used as one of the most important checks of the accounts. The trial balance, however, has lost its control function since the introduction of modern tools (particularly computers). In real life, the trial balance is no longer part of the eight-column financial statements.
  In this book the trial balance is just used as a tool to check the totals of the ledger accounts.
- The balance of the income statement, net income, is recorded in the debit column. This does not mean that equity is reduced: on the contrary. The credit total is higher, which means an increase in equity. The balance is recorded on the debit side to ensure equilibrium in the totals of the two columns.

Exercises

Answer sheet **3.1** Prepare the eight-column financial statements using the ledger accounts in exercise 2.2.

Answer sheet **3.2** Prepare the eight-column financial statements using the following data.

Figure 3.14

Account	Balances (in €)	
	Debit	Credit
Buildings	170,000	
Equipment	35,320	
Interest expenses	18,250	
Marketable securities	27,665	
Equity		144,240
Accounts receivable	57,310	
Accounts payable		69,145
Wages	38,780	
Tax payable		15,230
Inventories	50,845	
Energy expenses	2,365	
Gross profit		62,940
Various receivables	16,700	
Bank loan		31,870
Cash	1,695	
Various revenues and expenses		5,100
Depreciation costs	12,745	
Commission payable		650
Mortgage		102,500
	431,675	431,675

Answer sheet **3.3** A wholesaler in lemonades and liquors has prepared the following trial balance sheet:

Figure 3.15

		Trial balance (in €)	
No.	Account	Debit	Credit
1	Plant	150,000	
2	Buildings	1,040,000	40,300
3	Depreciation costs	56,881	
4	Housing costs	182,937	
5	Equipment	165,810	16,581
6	Office expenses	161,517	
7	9% mortgage		530,000
8	Interest expenses	47,700	
9	Wages	571,382	
10	Inventories, lemonade	1,880,437	1,805,833
11	Inventories, light liquors	2,101,771	1,994,402
12	Inventories, strong liquors	2,123,529	2,029,773
13	Advertising expenses	341,214	
14	Accounts receivable	6,269,117	6,099,312
15	Accounts payable	7,010,292	7,213,066
16	Discounts to customers	38,528	
17	Gross profit, lemonade	1,753	417,832
18	Gross profit, light liquors		635,188
19	Gross profit, strong liquors		533,902
20	Tax payable	1,836,714	1,860,031
21	Bank loan	13,467,831	13,817,418
22	Cash	41,373	38,515
23	Equity		473,655
24	Incidental revenues and expenses	17,935	913
		37,506,721	37,506,721

Prepare the full eight-column financial statements, using the information in the trial balance sheet.
Prepare the final balance sheet in two-column form, showing the debit accounts in order of increasing liquidity, and the credit accounts in order of increasing claims (liquidity balance sheet).

Closing the ledger accounts

Closing the accounts

Closing the accounts is a purely technical term: in manual accounting it is not done any more. At the start of a new accounting period the initial balance sheet will be opened, using the final balance sheet of the previous accounting period. Ledger accounts are not closed when intermediate financial statements are prepared, but are used for the remaining accounting period.

However, closing the accounts is an easy way to see which figures need to be recorded in the income statement and/or final balance sheet without preparing the eight-column financial statements. Closing the accounts is thus just helpful.

As an example we will use the 'inventories' ledger account in chapter 2.

■ Example 4.1

Figure 4.1

Debit			Inventories (in €)			Credit
Date	Description	Amount	Date	Description		Amount
01/01	Balance	20,000	05/01	On account		4,000
03/01	Purchased on account	5,000				

The balance of this account will be put on the side with the lowest total in order to balance the debit and credit sides (in equilibrium). The date will be the last date of the accounting period, in this case, 31 January. The description refers to where the balance will show in the eight-column financial statements: income statement or balance sheet.

Figure 4.2

Debit			Inventories (in €)				Credit
Date	Description		Amount	Date	Description		Amount
01/01	Balance		20,000	05/01	On account		4,000
03/01	Purchased on account		5,000	31/01	Balance		21,000
			25,000				25,000

The balance of €21,000 is also shown on the 'balances' and the final balance sheet in chapter 3, though on the debit side.

The balance on the ledger account is shown on the credit side because the debit side of the ledger account is €21,000 higher than the credit side. In this way the totals will be in equilibrium. Something similar was shown in chapter 3 when profit was calculated in the income statement.

When all other asset and liability accounts and all specialised equity accounts are closed in this way, the following is reached:

Figure 4.3

Debit			Accounts receivable (in €)				Credit
Date	Description		Amount	Date	Description		Amount
01/01	Balance		13,000	31/1	Balance		19,000
05/01	Products		6,000				
			19,000				19,000

Figure 4.4

Debit			Cash (in €)				Credit
Date	Description		Amount	Date	Description		Amount
01/01	Balance		6,000	04/01	Accounts payable		3,000
				06/01	Advertising expenses		500
				31/01	Balance		2,500
			6,000				6,000

Figure 4.5

Debit			Accounts payable (in €)				Credit
Date	Description		Amount	Date	Description		Amount
04/01	Cash		3,000	01/01	Balance		14,000
31/01	Balance		16,000	03/01	Inventories		5,000
			19,000				19,000

Figure 4.6

Debit			Gross profit (in €)				Credit
Date	Description		Amount	Date	Description		Amount
31/01	Income statement		2,000	05/01	Sales		2,000
			2,000				2,000

Figure 4.7

Debit			Advertising expenses (in €)				Credit
Date	Description		Amount	Date	Description		Amount
06/01	Cash		500	31/01	Income statement		500
			500				500

The 'equity' ledger account can be closed only after finishing the eight-column financial statements. In exercises, closing this account hardly ever happens.

First, profit is recorded on the ledger account and then the final balance is calculated. This figure is shown in the final balance sheet as new equity.

Figure 4.8

Debit			Equity (in €)				Credit
Date	Description		Amount	Date	Description		Amount
31/01	Balance sheet		26,500	01/01	Balance		25,000
				31/01	Profit		1,500
			26,500				26,500

Summarising the six accounting rules:
Accounting rule 1: an increase in assets is debited to an asset account.
Accounting rule 2: an increase in liability/debt is credited to a liability/debt account.
Accounting rule 3: a decrease in assets is credited to an asset account.
Accounting rule 4: a decrease in liability/debt is debited to a liability/debt account.
Accounting rule 5: an increase in equity is credited to a specialised equity account.
Accounting rule 6: a decrease in equity is debited to a specialised equity account.

Remarks:
- For all financial facts there is written evidence, such as purchase receipts and sales invoices, cash receipts, etc. For internal financial facts, such as depreciation, internal documents will be written.
- Each financial transaction is debited and credited for the same total amount, resulting in equilibrium in the ledger: the total debit amounts of all the accounts equal the total credit amounts.
- Specialised equity accounts will be created for various expenses, such as labour costs, maintenance costs, rent, etc. This shows clearly what sort of expenses have been made. The 'various expenses' account will only be used incidentally.
- In the case of new assets or new liabilities (e.g. a new loan), a new ledger account with a matching name will be created (in this case 'loan').

Exercises

4.1 Close the ledger accounts in exercise 4.1, including the account 'equity', per 31 January. Show the number of the account 'withdrawal' separate from profit on the account 'equity'.

4.2 Close the ledger accounts in exercise 4.2, including the account 'equity'.

Journal entries

The paper on which you make journal entries is nothing more than some 'scrap paper' indicating which figures need to be recorded on ledger accounts: debit or credit.
In the past, journal entries were an important control tool. Today modern equipment has made them superfluous.
A journal entry is made for each financial fact. In chapter 2 it stated that for each transaction ledger accounts were debited and credited for the same total amount. This means that each journal entry on our 'scrap paper' needs to be in equilibrium, which is why our 'scrap paper' is a great help in the accounting process.
In most exercises students are required only to make journal entries, assuming that the student, as well as knowing how the journal entry is made, is also familiar with how it is processed in the ledger accounts.

The paper for journal entries looks like this:

Figure 5.1

Date	Ledger account	Debit	Credit

When a ledger account needs to be credited, its name is written slightly to the right. This is because the relevant figure will be recorded in the 'credit' column. This procedure is very effective in answering questions such as:

How do you record a purchase invoice ?

Answer: Inventories;
          Accounts payable.

Without mentioning the figure it is clear that the 'inventories' ledger account is debited and the 'accounts payable' ledger account is credited (its name is written slightly to the right).

It is obvious that the six accounting rules outlined in chapter 2 need to be applied when making journal entries.

Example 5.1

3 January	Purchased on account products with a value of €5,000.
4 January	Paid cash to a supplier, €3,000.
5 January	Sold products on account for €6,000. The purchase price was €4,000.
6 January	Paid cash for advertising expenses, €500.

The journal entries are as follows:

Figure 5.2

Date	Ledger account (in €)	Debit	Credit
03/01	Inventories	5,000	
	Accounts payable		5,000
04/01	Accounts payable	3,000	
	Cash		3,000
05/01	Accounts receivable	6,000	
	Inventories		4,000
	Gross profit		2,000
06/01	Advertising expenses	500	
	Cash		500

After all journal entries have been made, the ledger accounts will be adjusted. The ledger accounts will then be the same as those in chapter 2.

Figure 5.3

Debit			Inventories (in €)			Credit
Date	Description	Amount	Date	Description		Amount
01/01	Balance	20,000	05/01	Sold on account		4,000
03/01	Purchased on account	5,000				

5 Journal entries 39

Figure 5.4

Debit		Accounts receivable (in €)				Credit
Date	Description	Amount	Date	Description	Amount	
01/01	Balance	13,000				
05/01	Products	6,000				

Figure 5.5

Debit		Cash (in €)				Credit
Date	Description	Amount	Date	Description	Amount	
01/01	Balance	6,000	04/01	Accounts payable	3,000	
			06/01	Advertising expenses	500	

Figure 5.6

Debit		Equity (in €)				Credit
Date	Description	Amount	Date	Description	Amount	
01/01	Balance	25,000				

Figure 5.7

Debit		Accounts payable (in €)				Credit
Date	Description	Amount	Date	Description	Amount	
04/01	Cash	3,000	01/01	Balance	14,000	
			03/01	Products	5,000	

Figure 5.8

Debit		Gross profit (in €)				Credit
Date	Description	Amount	Date	Description	Amount	
05/01	Sales	2,000				

Figure 5.9

Debit			Advertising expenses (in €)			Credit
Date	Description	Amount	Date	Description		Amount
06/01	Cash	500				

Remark:
Ledger accounts always need to be opened with the balances (if applicable). This must be done before financial facts occur.

The accounting scheme is as follows:

Figure 5.10

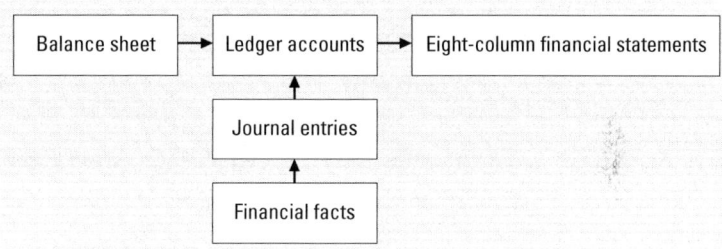

Exercises

5.1 Prepare the journal entries from the data in exercise 2.2 and check the ledger accounts afterwards.

5.2 (Data from this exercise will also be used in exercises 6.2, 7.2 and 8.1).

Mr. A.van Nugen works 20 hours per week as controller in a medium-sized manufacturing plant. In addition he has a wholesale business in computer equipment. He limits himself to trading one kind of computer and screen for advanced graphic applications, purchased at Compu-Import JSC, and one sort of printer, purchased at Print-Tech JSC. He distributes these products to various retailers and dealers in office equipment.

He also purchases trade-in equipment from his customers, which he sells directly to private individuals. Buying the trade-in equipment is done just to 'tie' his customers. The selling price of this equipment equals the purchase price.

Trade-in equipment is sold cash only; all other sales and purchases are on account.

As at 1 September 2009 Mr. Van Nugen's wholesale business has the following data:

Figure 5.11

Debit		Balance sheet 1 September 2009 (in €)		Credit
Equipment	15,800	Equity		16,350
Inventories	15,100	Loan		16,500
Trade-in equipment	1,000	Accounts payable		5,750
Accounts receivable	7,300	Bank loan		1,200
Cash	600			
	39,800			39,800

List of inventories (in €):
5 PCs at 2,000	10,000
7 screens at 500	3,500
4 printers at 400	1,600
	15,100
Trade-in equipment	1,000

List of accounts receivable:
Facet Stationer's	4,230
Hardware Store	3,070
	7,300

List of accounts payable:
Print-Tech JSC	2,400
Compu-Import JSC	3,350
	5,750

Mr. Van Nugen uses the following specialised equity accounts:
Gross profit
Various office expenses
Rent
Advertising expenses
Depreciation expenses
Interest expenses.

The following financial facts occurred in September 2009 (in €):

02/09	Purchased from Compu-Import JSC:			
	3 PCs at 2,000		6,000	
	2 screens at 500		1,000	
				7,000
	Invoice I-39 received today, as well as the products			
04/09	Cash received from Facet Stationers according to B-65			4,230
05/09	Sold on account to Facet Stationers:			
	3 PCs at 2,700		8,100	
	3 screens at 700		2,100	
	2 printers at 675		1,350	
			11,550	
	Purchased as a special offer:			
	2 PCs, 1 screen and 1 printer		2,500 –	
				9,050
	Sales invoice V-47, as well as the products, has been sent today			
06/09	Sold trade-in equipment, on sale 01/09 (according to K-60)			1,000
06/09	Paid cash for advertising in local newspaper (K-61)			200
09/09	Purchased on account from Print-Tech JSC:			
	3 printers at 400			1,200
	Products and purchase invoice I-40 received today			

10/09	Paid various office expenses, in cash, according to K-62			150
11/09	Purchased on account from Compu-Import JSC:			
	5 PCs at 2,000		10,000	
	4 screens at 500		2,000	
				12,000
	Products and invoice I-41 received today			
12/09	Sold on account to Hardware Store:			
	2 PCs at 2,700		5,400	
	3 screens at 700		2,100	
	1 printer at 675		675	
			8,175	
	Purchased products in special offer for		500 –	
				7,675
	Invoice V-48 and products sent today			
13/09	Sold trade-in equipment for cash			700
13/09	Purchased a desk and received invoice I-42 from Kantoorinrichting LLC			2,350
14/09	Received cash from Hardware Store, according to B-66			5,000
17/09	Paid cash (B-67) to:			
	Print-Tech JSC		2,400	
	Compu-Import JSC		10,000	
				12,400
18/09	Paid cash for publicity leaflets (K-64)			700
20/09	Hardware Store returned 2 damaged screens today Credit invoice V-49 sent today			1,400
23/09	Received cash from Facet Stationer's (B-68)			5,000
24/09	Returned to Compu-Import JSC two damaged screens Credit invoice I-43 received today			1,000
25/09	Paid cash monthly rent for warehouse and office (B-69)			2,500
26/09	Sold on account to Brederoo Company:			
	4 PCs at 2,700		10,800	
	3 printers at 675		2,025	
				12,825
	Products and invoice V-50 sent today			
26/09	Purchased an office chair, paid cash (K-65)			500
27/09	Paid cash to Compu-Import JSC (B-70)			4,500

30/09	Paid cash (B-71):	
	Redemption on loan	1,500
	Interest on loan	660
		2,160

30/09	Monthly depreciation on equipment (D-17)	320

a Prepare journal entries for the above financial facts.

b On the basis of the journal entries, prepare the following ledger accounts: cash, inventories, accounts receivable, accounts payable, and bank loan (Careful opening the accounts!) and close them as at 30 September.

5.3 Mr. W. Geraards buys and sells tree-trunks that can be used as garden walls. He sells both to garden centres and to private individuals. When somebody orders, Mr. Geraards looks for an importer or forestry company that can supply trunks of the right thickness. Afterwards, the trunks are cut in a saw-mill to the right length. The sawed trunks are then stored in a shed until the order needs to be delivered.

The following financial facts occurred in March 2009:

02/03	Paid rent in cash for March, for the shed and the office		2,750
04/03	Received invoice for supply of trunks, already stored in shed		13,670
05/03	Received invoice from the saw-mill for sawing the above		1,200
10/03	Paid cash to a supplier	7,390	
	Paid cash to the saw-mill	870	
			8,260
19/03	Sent invoice for sawed trunks		8,500
	Purchase price was 7,000		
23/03	Received cash from a customer	8,500	
	Cash discount	170	
			8,330
27/03	Paid freight costs in cash		250
30/03	Paid gas company invoice in cash		120

Prepare journal entries for the above data and create names or ledger accounts.

Special journals

Chapter 5 showed how financial facts are recorded in ledger accounts via journal entries. Just a small number of financial facts were displayed. In reality, however, a small company needs to record dozens of financial facts daily, and a large company hundreds more complicated facts. It is obvious that this way of recording makes ledger accounts less than transparent.

Journals

To solve this problem, accounting documents that are similar, for instance all purchase invoices, are collected in special journals each accounting period, after which they are recorded together in one journal entry as if there were just one purchase invoice.
In this course only the following special journals will be used:
- purchase book
- sales book
- cash book
- general journal.

In practice, there are many more special journals: one can be made for any similar accounting documents that will be recorded in the journal at the same time.
Special journals can fall into two categories: without and with the capacity to control.

Purchase book
Sales book

The first category includes the purchase book and the sales book.
The general journal, also in category one, will be discussed later.
The purchase and sales books may look as follows:

Figure 6.1

Purchase book

1	2	3	4	5	6	7
Date	No.	Accounts payable	Total	Products	Other	Account

The columns speak for themselves: in the first column the invoice date (or the date on which the invoice was received) is recorded; the second column the internal invoice number, assigned by the company itself to a purchase invoice, i.e. not the supplier's invoice number. The third column shows the name of the supplier; the fourth column the total figure on the invoice; the fifth column the value of products available for sales, thus increasing the inventories. Columns six and seven are meant for products (or services) not available for sales: column 5 will then be omitted, the amount will be recorded in column 6 and column 7 will show the ledger account in which the amount in column 6 needs to be recorded.

The purchase book can have as many columns as the company wishes and must include those data needed to make the right journal entry. In chapter 9, for instance, which discusses VAT, an extra column will be added.

Figure 6.2

Sales book

1	2	3	4	5	6	7
Date	No.	Accounts receivable	Total	Purchase price	Other	Account

The first four columns have identical data to the first four columns in the purchase book. The fifth column shows the purchase price of the products, the cost of goods sold. The difference between the fourth and the fifth column is the gross profit. Column six shows the book value of products incidentally sold, such as equipment, etc. The difference between the fourth and the sixth column is incidental profit or loss. The last column contains the name of the ledger account in which the figure in column six is recorded. If columns 6 and 7 are used, nothing will be recorded in column 5.

Here also, different and more extensive classifications are possible; chapter 9 will show an example in which VAT is included.

Purchase and sales invoices are recorded daily in the special journals. When the accounting period is finished, usually after one month, the special journals are closed, which means that the figures in the various columns will be added up. Then the journal entry will be prepared as if it were one invoice.

■ **Example 6.1**

A firm received the following purchase and sales invoices in April.

02/04   Received invoice I-65 from Dalen Company, for products purchased for €6,000

07/04   Sent invoice V-88 to Hoogenwerf LLC for delivered products. Sales price €4,000; cost of goods sold €2,500

12/04 Received invoice I-66 from Kantoorhandel Vis for stationery purchased for €245

19/04 Sent invoice V-89 for products sold to Gradulus Company. Sales price €8,100, cost of goods sold €5,700

20/04 Received invoice I-67 from Bartels JSC for products purchased for €2,300

22/04 Sent invoice V-90 to Hagendoorn Company for trade-in machinery. This machinery had a book value of €1,200 and was also sold for €1,200.

Figure 6.3

Purchase book (in €)

1	2	3	4	5	6	7
Date	No.	Accounts payable	Total	Products	Other	Account
02/04	I-65	Dalen Company	6,000	6,000	245	Office expenses
12/04	I-66	Kantoorhandel Vis	245			
20/04	I-67	Bartles JSC	2,300	2,300		
		Total	8,545	8,300	245	

Figure 6.4

Sales book (in €)

1	2	3	4	5	6	7
Date	No.	Accounts receivable	Total	Purchase price	Other	Account
07/04	V-88	Hoogenwerf LLC	4,000	2,500		
19/04	V-89	Gradulus Company	8,100	5,700		
22/04	V-90	Hagendoorn Company	1,200		1,200	Machinery
		Total	13,300	8,200	1,200	

At the end of the month one journal entry will be made in the purchase journal instead of three (in €):

30/04	Inventories	8,300	
	Office expenses	245	
	Accounts payable		8,545

Same procedure for the sales book:

30/04	Accounts receivable	13,300	
	Inventories		8,200
	Machinery		1,200
	Gross profit		3,900

After these journal entries have been recorded in the ledger, the relevant ledger accounts will show only one line instead of three. In the case of monthly closing of the special journals, this means just 12 lines per account per year. This makes it easier to prepare the balances in the eight-column financial statements.

The consecutive numbering in the special journals is another advantage since it is easy to see whether an invoice has been omitted. If detailed information about a certain invoice is required, the special journals clearly show which name is linked to each invoice, which makes it possible to find the relevant invoice in the archives.

The cash book is the second special journal with control functions.

In the cash book all cash receipts and cash payment slips are recorded. This is why the cash book has two sides – debit and credit – in contrast with the purchase and sales books.

Figure 6.5

Debit				Cash book				Credit
Date	No.	Account	Amount	Date	No.	Account	Amount	

Cash receipts are recorded on the debit side (accounting rule 1: increase of an asset is debited) and cash payments on the credit side (accounting rule 3: decrease of an asset is credited). These accounting rules were discussed in chapter 2.

The classification in the cash book is similar to that in the 'cash' ledger account. The difference, however, is substantial: the cash book assembles all the financial facts that lead to a change in the asset cash. At the end of the accounting period, totals are recorded in journal entries, after which the totals are transferred to the 'cash' ledger account. All ledger accounts together create a new balance sheet via the eight-column financial statements discussed in chapter 3.

It may be clear that the 'cash' ledger account can only be debited or credited with figures from the cash book.

The ' account' column is important in the cash book. It contains the name of the ledger account in which the relevant figure needs to be recorded as well. Journal entries consist of debit and credit entries.

Example 6.2

30/04   Paid cash for printing propaganda leaflets, €500 (K-36).

Apart from recording the 'cash' ledger account, an entry needs to be made in a specialised equity account (expenses: decrease in equity, see chapter 2). In this case, we want to debit 'advertising expenses'. The name of this ledger account is the description in the cash book, to avoid searching for the ledger accounts in the journal entry at the end of the accounting period.

Figure 6.6

Debit				Cash book (in €)				Credit
Date	No.	Account	Amount	Date	No.	Account	Amount
				30/04	K-36	Advertising expenses	500

If this is the only entry in the cash book, the journal entry will look as follows (in €):

30/04   Advertising expenses   500
            Cash   500

In practice, the cash book is updated daily, after which the accounting slips (receipts and payment slips) are filed. If the description in the special journals differs from the name of the relevant ledger account, all accounting documents need to be checked before the journal entry can be made. This means a double workload.

Example 6.3

30/04   Sold cash products for €600. Cost of goods sold €450 (K-37)

The 'cash' ledger account 'cash' needs to be debited, and the 'inventories' and 'gross profit' ledger accounts need to be credited. (accounting rules 3 and 5, see chapter 2). On the debit side of the cash book, the total figure, €600, needs to be split into two figures: decrease in inventories €450 and gross profit €150.

Figure 6.7

Debit				Cash book (in €)				Credit
Date	No.	Account	Amount	Date	No.	Account	Amount
30/4	K-37	Inventories Gross profit	450 150				

Date and number of the accounting document need to be noted only once.

If this is the only entry in the cash book, the journal entry would be as follows (in €):

30/04	Cash	600	
	Inventories		450
	Gross profit		150

Another difference from the purchase and sales books is the cash book's initial balance.
This balance shows available cash at the start of the accounting period (a negative cash balance will appear as a bank loan on the credit side). At the end of the accounting period, a new balance will be determined, which can be compared with the available cash. This is an important control tool. On 1 January, the initial balance in the cash book needs to be equal to the figure on the balance sheet as at 1 January. In general, small companies prepare a balance sheet once or twice per year. Monthly closing of the cash book means monthly control.

■ **Example 6.4**

On 1 April a company had a cash balance of €725.
In that month the following financial facts relating to cash occurred:

02/04   K-46 Sold cash products for €800, cost of goods sold, €600

05/04   K-47 Paid creditor Jansen, €500

11/04   K-48 Received from debtor Wolters, €350

15/04   K-49 Paid for advertising in the local newspaper, €125

18/04   K-50 Sold products for €720, cost of goods sold €570

24/04   K-51 Received from debtor Hendriks, €250

27/04   K-52 Paid to supplier Verdegaal, €680

30/04   K-53 Paid repair costs for the truck, €450

Figure 6.8

Debit				Cash book (in €)				Credit
Date	No.	Account	Amount	Date	No.	Account		Amount
01/04		Balance	725	05/04	K-47	Accounts payable		500
02/04	K-46	Inventories	600	15/04	K-49	Advertising expenses		125
		Gross profit	200	27/04	K-52	Accounts payable		680
11/04	K-48	Accounts receivable	350	30/04	K-53	Car expenses		450
18/04	K-50	Inventories	570	30/04		Balance		1,090
		Gross profit	150					
24/04	K-51	Accounts receivable	250					
		Total	2,845			Total		2,845

The cash balance as at 30/04, €1,090, needs to be equal to the available cash in the firm. As in chapter 4, when closing the ledger accounts, the balance is inserted in the column with the lowest total in order to balance debit and credit totals. A final balance on the credit side means that the initial balance plus cash receipts is higher than the cash payments. The following accounting period will be opened on the debit side with a balance of €1,090.

Two separate journal entries will be made, one for the debit side and one for the credit side. Figures to be recorded in the same ledger account can be added.
Total cash receipts can be calculated by deducting the initial balance from the total. Total cash payments equal the total minus the final balance.

Journal entry on the debit side (in €):
30/04   Cash (2,845 – 725)   2,120
            Inventories   1,170
            Gross profit   350
            Accounts receivable   600

Journal entry on the credit side:
30/04   Accounts payable   1,180
            Advertising expenses   125
            Car expenses   450
                Cash (2,845 – 1,090)   1,755

The difference between the debit and the credit entries on the 'cash' ledger account is the change in the cash balance, in this case €365 (1,090 – 725). ■

Since all similar accounting documents are first collected in special journals and entries in the same ledger accounts are added up, the number of entries in the ledger is considerably reduced.
The name of the special journal in which the fact has been recorded is mentioned as description in the ledger. This makes the ledger transparent and it will be easy to find details in the relevant special journal. Via the number of the accounting document in the special journal, this document can be found in the archives.
The use of special journals is called the method of collective transfers.

General journal

The last special journal is the general journal, in which all financial facts are recorded that cannot be entered in one of the other special journals. Broadly it concerns internal accounting documents. Collective entries are not possible in this case since the general journal concerns a variety of different facts of which individual journal entries will be made. The layout of the general journal is very simple:

Figure 6.9

General journal

Date	No.	Description	Amount

The 'description' column will have all the data needed to make the journal entry. In this way the general journal functions as a special journal and, at the same time, as an internal accounting document.

Example 6.5

On 17 April it appeared that products with a value of €100 were stolen from the warehouse
On 23 April the firm agreed with the trustee of a bankrupt customer to remit a debt of €350. The trustee has been informed in writing
Monthly depreciation on equipment is €750

Figure 6.10

General journal (in €)

Date	No.	Description	Amount
17/4	D-11	Stolen products	100
23/4	D-12	Customer debt remitted	350
30/4	D-13	Depreciation of equipment	750

The following three journal entries will be made (in €):

30/04	Various revenues and expenses	100	
	Inventories		100
30/04	Various revenues and expenses	350	
	Accounts receivable		350
30/04	Depreciation expenses	750	
	Equipment		750

The accounting scheme is nearly complete:

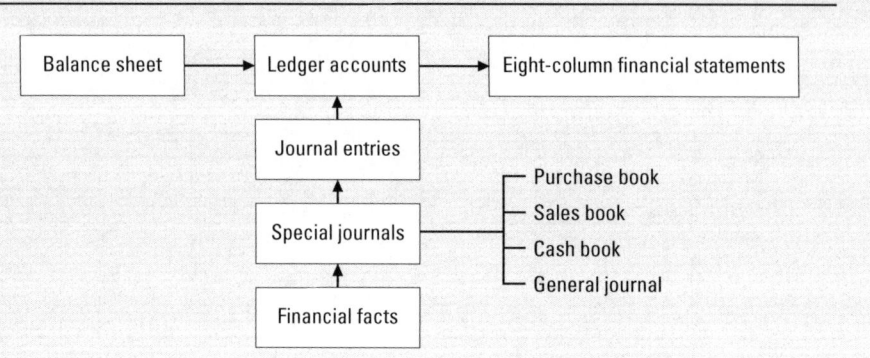

Figure 6.11

Remarks
- An accounting document can only be entered in a special journal once. If entries are made in more special journals, then more identical entries will, via the journal entries, be made in the ledger.
- Only purchases and sales on account are recorded in the purchase journal and the sales journal.
- Purchase and sales credit invoices can be recorded in various ways. If there are many credit notes, it may be wise to create special journals: a credit purchase journal and/or a credit sales journal. The journal entries are exactly the opposite of the journal entries in the purchase and sales journal. In the case of just a few credit invoices, one can either enter a remark in the general journal or record the figures negatively in the purchase or sales journal. This violates the accounting rules (never record negative numbers), but in this case it is recommended to make calculations easier. To avoid mistakes, it must be very clear that a negative entry is being made: use -/- or write the figure and text in red.

Exercises

6.1 Verguson Company in Nieuwegein buys and sells linen cupboards of the following three types (in €):

Type	Characteristics	Purchase price	Selling price
A	No shelves	1,250	1,500
B	Half shelves	1,475	1,770
C	Two drawers	1,540	1,850

Purchase and sales invoices are always received/sent with the products.
The following data refer to October 2009:

01 October	Cash balance		12,830
03 October	Received invoice I-612 from Aris furniture factory in Apeldoorn for the delivery of 5 type A cupboards		6,250
07 October	Sent invoice V-738 to Woonpaleis in Zeist for the supply of:		
	2 type A cupboards	3,000	
	1 type C cupboards	1,850	4,850
10 October	Received from Peters JSC in Nieuwegein invoice I-613 for the delivery of new office equipment		15,000
12 October	Cash received from JSC Herwijnen (B-58) for payment of invoice V-732		9,890
13 October	Sent invoice V-739 to De Boer Meubelen in Utrecht for the delivery of:		
	3 type B cupboards	5,310	
	3 type C cupboards	5,550	10,860
16 October	Paid the energy bill for October in cash (B-59)		578
17 October	Paid cash (B-60) to Haversma LLC, invoice I-608		13,535
18 October	Received from Haversma LLC invoice I-614 for the delivery of:		
	3 type B cupboards	4,425	
	5 type C cupboards	7,700	12,125

21 October	Sent invoice V-740 to Herwijnen for supplying:		
	2 type A cupboards	3,000	
	2 type B cupboards	3,540	
	2 type C cupboards	3,700	
			10,240
23 October	Sent invoice V-741 to H. Versluis for taking over the old office equipment, which had a book value of 1,500		1,200
25 October	Paid cash (B-610) to Peters JSC, invoice I-613		15,000
26 October	Received invoice I-615 from Geerling transport company for freight expenses in the first two weeks of October		1,800
28 October	Cash received (B-26) in payment of invoice V-738, Woonpaleis		4,850
30 October	Sent invoice V-742 to Woonplezier LLC, Bussum, for the delivery of:		
	1 type A cupboard	1,500	
	1 type B cupboard	1,770	
	3 type C cupboard	5,550	
			8,820
31 October	Paid in cash (B-63) rent of the warehouse for October		2,500
31 October	Equipment depreciation expenses for October (D-117)		300

Answer sheet **6.1 a** Prepare and close the special journals.
b Make the journal entries of the special journals.

Answer sheet **6.2 a** Using the data of exercise 5.2, prepare and close the special journals.
b Prepare the journal entries.
Answer sheet **c** Prepare and close, on the basis of the journal entries, the following ledger accounts: cash, inventories, accounts receivable and accounts payable.
d Compare the number of entries and the balances with the ledger accounts in exercise 5.2.
e Compare the balance of the cash book with the balance of the 'cash' ledger account.

6.3 Debbie Klovers Company shows the following totals at the end of May (in €):

Cash book debit side:
Accounts receivable	29,340
Loan	2,000
Interest	150

Cash book credit side:
Accounts payable	15,330
Energy expenses	400
Rent	1,700
Advertising expenses	250
Office expenses	75
Wages	1,200
Maintenance costs	650

Purchase journal:
'Totals' column	21,310
'Products' column	18,160
'Various' column (equipment)	2,520
'Various' column (advertising)	630

Sales journal:
'Totals' column	20,930
'Products' column	17,360

General journal:
Depreciation of equipment	250
Missing products	630

Prepare the journal entries.

Sub-ledger accounts

In chapter 6 we learned that the cash book can be used regularly to check currently available cash. This should equal the balance in the cash book. This check can be done at the end of each month, when closing the special journals, without needing to close the ledger. Other issues in the accounting process may require our attention. For example, the 'accounts receivable' ledger account. The balance of this account shows the total receivables from customers. It is, however, desirable to know the amount by customer and the age of the receivable. This can be done by splitting up the ledger account into one account per debtor, the accounts receivable sub-ledger. At the end of each accounting period the total balances of these sub-ledger accounts needs to equal the balance on the 'accounts receivable' ledger account.

Accounts receivable sub-ledger

These accounts receivable sub-ledger accounts can have the following format:

Figure 7.1

Name				
Date	Accounting document	Debit	Credit	Balance

The name of the accounts receivable sub-ledger is the same as the name of the debtor. The columns 'date' and 'accounting document' need no further explanation.
There are no debit and credit sides, but the columns 'debit ' and 'credit' have the same function. An advantage is that the balance of the receivable from each debtor can be seen directly after making the entry. The sub-ledger accounts do not need to be closed separately.

Sometimes the 'balance' column is missing; the balance will then be calculated by closing the accounts at the end of the accounting period, in the same way as closing the cash book.

Here also, the accounting rules discussed in chapter 2 can be applied unabridged. Since only the accounting of receivables is recorded, accounting rule 1 (increase in assets) and 3 (decrease in assets) are applicable.

To ensure that the balances in the accounts receivable sub-ledger equal the balance of the 'accounts receivable' ledger account, all entries in the 'accounts receivable' ledger account, made via special journals and journal entries, must be recorded in the sub-ledger as well.

Chapter 2 described how, in a manual accounting system, all ledger accounts are separate cards. This is also the case for the sub-ledger. For each sub-ledger, an individual card will be filed.

The following example shows how these entries are made.

■ **Example 7.1**

The balance sheet as at 1 January shows the following, among others (in €): Accounts receivable €3,600.

The following debtors are registered:
Jansen Company	1,500
Pietersen Company	2,100
	3,600

The 'accounts receivable' ledger account is opened as follows (in €):

Figure 7.2

Debit			Accounts receivable			Credit
Date	Description	Amount	Date	Description		Amount
01/01	Balance	3,600				

At the same time the accounts receivable sub-ledger will be opened (in €):

Accounts receivable sub-ledger

Figure 7.3

Name	Jansen Company				
Date	Accounting document		Debit	Credit	Balance
01/01	Balance				1,500

Figure 7.4

Name	Pietersen Company			
Date	Accounting document	Debit	Credit	Balance
01/01	Balance			2,100

After opening, the totals of the sub-ledger equal the total of the ledger account. ■

■ **Example 7.2**

03/01   Sold products to Jansen Company for €1,200. Cost of goods sold €850. Invoice V-01 and products have been despatched today.

This financial fact will be recorded in the sales book (in €):

Figure 7.5

Sales book (in €)

Date	No.	Accounts receivable	Total	Cost of goods sold	Other	Account
01/03	V-01	Jansen Company	1,200	850		

Since this transaction influences the balance of accounts receivable, an entry will be made in the accounts receivable sub-ledger (in €):

Accounts receivable sub-ledger

Figure 7.6

Name	Jansen Company			
Date	Accounting document	Debit	Credit	Balance
01/01	Balance			1,500
03/01	V-01	1,200		2,700

Figure 7.7

Name	Pietersen Company			
Date	Accounting document	Debit	Credit	Balance
01/01	Balance			2,100

Assuming that this is the only sales invoice in January, the following journal entry can be made in the sales journal at the end of the month:

31/01	Accounts receivable	1,200	
	Inventories		850
	Gross profit		350

After entering in the ledger, 'accounts receivable' shows the following (in €):

Figure 7.8

Debit			Accounts receivable			Credit
Date	Description	Amount	Date	Description	Amount
01/01	Balance	3,600			
31/01	Sales book	1,200			

The balance in the ledger account, €4,800, equals the balances in the sub-ledger, €2,700 + 2,100. ▪

■ **Example 7.3**

05/01   Paid cash (B-01) by Pietersen Company, €700

The balance as at 01/01 amounted to €5,800. The entry in the cash book is as follows (in €):

Figure 7.9

Debit				Cash book				Credit
Date	No.	Account	Amount	Date	No.	Account	Amount
01/01		Balance	5,800				
05/01	B-01	Accounts receivable	700				

The entry in the accounts receivable sub-ledger (in €):

Accounts receivable sub-ledger

Figure 7.10

Name: Jansen Company

Date	Accounting document	Debit	Credit	Balance
01/01	Balance			1,500
03/01	V-01	1,200		2,700

Figure 7.11

Name: Pietersen Company

Date	Accounting document	Debit	Credit	Balance
01/01	Balance			2,100
05/01	B-01		700	1,400

Again assuming that this is the only document in January, the following journal entry will be made after closing the cash book (in €):

```
31/01   Cash                              700
            Accounts receivable                    700
```

After adjusting the ledger, the 'accounts receivable' account looks as follows:

Figure 7.12

Debit			Accounts receivable (in €)			Credit
Date	Description	Amount	Date	Description		Amount
01/01	Balance	3,600	31/01	Cash book		700
31/01	Sales book	1,200				

Here also, the balance of the 'accounts receivable' ledger account (€4,100) equals the total balances in the accounts receivable sub-ledger (€2,700 + 1,400). ■

Accounts receivable sub-ledger

Accounts payable sub-ledger

Inventories sub-ledger

Apart from the accounts receivable sub-ledger there are also the 'accounts payable sub-ledger' and the 'inventories sub-ledger'. The accounts payable sub-ledger is identical to the accounts receivable sub-ledger: however, there is a credit balance, which, of course, equals the credit balance in the 'accounts payable' ledger account.

Only accounting rules 2 (increase in debt) and 4 (decrease of debt), discussed in chapter 2, will be applied.
The inventories sub-ledger has, in general, a different outline:

Figure 7.13

Name

Date	No.	Received from/Delivered to	Received	Delivered	Inventory

The name of the account is the name of one of the products in total inventories. The third column gives the name of the supplier of the relevant product or the name of the customer. The 'received' column corresponds with the 'debit' column in the other sub-ledgers; the 'delivered' column corresponds with the 'credit' column and the 'inventory' column equals the 'balance' column.
Accounting rules 1 and 3, discussed in chapter 2, apply here.
The 'delivered' column shows the cost of goods sold. This corresponds with the entry in the 'inventories' ledger account derived from the sales journal.

■ Example 7.4

The balance sheet as at 1 January shows, among others, the following data (in €):

Inventories 6,500

This inventory consists of:

Product A	1,900
Product B	2,800
Product C	1,800
	6,500

7 Sub-ledger accounts

After the ledger is opened the 'inventories' ledger account shows the following (in €):

Figure 7.14

Debit			Inventories			Credit
Date	Description	Amount	Date	Description		Amount
01/01	Balance	6,500				

The inventories sub-ledger, after opening (in €):

Inventories sub-ledger

Figure 7.15

Name Product A

Date	No.	Received from/Delivered to	Received	Delivered	Inventory
01/01		Balance			1,900

Figure 7.16

Name Product B

Date	No.	Received from/Delivered to	Received	Delivered	Inventory
01/01		Balance			2,800

Figure 7.17

Name Product C

Date	No.	Received from/Delivered to	Received	Delivered	Inventory
01/01		Balance			1,800

Here also, it appears that, directly after opening, the total balances in the 'inventories' column in the sub-ledger equals the balance of the 'inventories' ledger account.

Example 7.5

02/01   Purchased from Klaassen Company (in €):

Product A	750
Product B	500
	1,250

Invoice I-01 and products have been received today.

This financial fact will be recorded in the purchase journal, as well as in the accounts payable sub-ledger, in the account of Klaassen Company (in the credit column €1,250: the column 'balance' increases by €1,250).

The influence on inventories will be shown in the inventories sub-ledger (in €):

Inventories sub-ledger

Figure 7.18

Name Product A

Date	No.	Received from/Delivered to	Received	Delivered	Inventory
01/01		Balance	750		1,900
01/01	I-01	Klaassen Company			2,650

Figure 7.19

Name Product B

Date	No.	Received from/Delivered to	Received	Delivered	Inventory
01/02		Balance			2,800
01/02	I-01	Klaassen Company	500		3,300

Figure 7.20

Name Product C

Date	No.	Received from/Delivered to	Received	Delivered	Inventory
01/01		Balance			1,800

If no further purchase invoices will be received, the following journal entry is made at the end of the month (in €):

31/01	Inventories	1,250	
	Accounts payable		1,250

The 'inventories' ledger account will then appear as follows (in €):

Figure 7.21

Debit			Inventories			Credit
Date	Description	Amount	Date	Description		Amount
01/01	Balance	6,500				
31/01	Purchase book	1,250				

The balance of the ledger account, €7,750, is equal to the totals in the sub-ledger (€2,650 + 3,300 + 1,800). ■

■ **Example 7.6**

06/01	Sold to Hendriksen Company (in €):	
	Product A (purchase price 1,000)	1,300
	Product B (purchase price 300)	500
		1,800

Sales invoice V-01 has been sent, as well as the products.

This invoice will be recorded in the sales journal and in the accounts receivable sub-ledger in the account of Hendriksen Company.
The following adjustments will be made in the inventories sub-ledger:

Inventories sub-ledger (in €)

Figure 7.22

Name Product A

Date	No.	Received from/Delivered to	Received	Delivered	Inventory
01/01		Balance	750		1,900
02/01	I-01	Klaassen Company			2,650
06/01	V-01	Hendriksen Company		1,000	1,650

Figure 7.23

Name Product B

Date	No.	Received from/Delivered to	Received	Delivered	Inventory
01/01		Balance			2,800
02/01	I-01	Klaassen Company	500		3,300

Figure 7.24

Name Product C

Date	No.	Received from/Delivered to	Received	Delivered	Inventory
01/01		Balance			1,800
06/01	V-01	Hendriksen Company		300	1,500

The following journal entry is made, based on the sales journal (there are no other sales invoices) (in €):

31/01	Accounts receivable	1,800	
	Inventories		1,300
	Gross profit		500

The ledger account appears as follows (in €):

Figure 7.25

Debit			Inventories			Credit
Date	Description	Amount		Date	Description	Amount
01/01	Balance	6,500		31/01	Sales journal	1,300
31/01	Purchase book	1,250				

Here also, the total balances in the inventories sub-ledger (€1,650 + 3,300 + 1,500) equal the balance on the ledger account (€6,450). ∎

The complete accounting scheme is as follows:

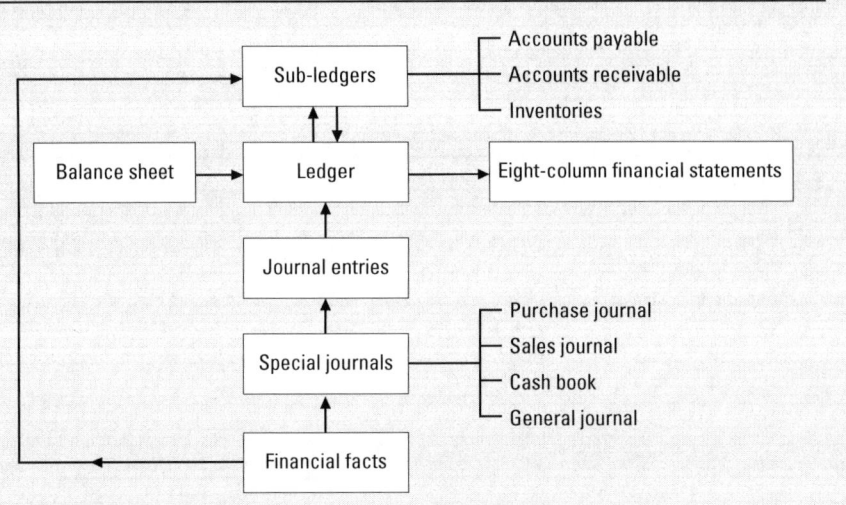

Figure 7.26

Remarks
- In this book only the three sub-ledgers mentioned are discussed. In practice there can be more: the accounting procedure is exactly the same.
- For any new supplier, customer or product a new sub-ledger account is made. Compare how a new asset or debt is recorded in the ledger (chapter 2).
- An accounting document can be entered once in a special journal, but one document can result in more than one entry in various sub-ledgers, and sometimes no entry needs to be made in a sub-ledger. It does not matter which special journal is used: as soon as the balance of accounts receivable, accounts payable or inventories changes, one or more entries in the sub-ledgers will follow.
- It is not possible to follow the whole accounting process in each exercise. In general, one only has to prepare parts, for instance:
  - cash book only
  - purchase journal plus one of the accounts in the accounts payable sub-ledger
  - part of the eight-column financial statements.

In textbooks that follow this introductory course, preparing journal entries will usually be required, just to keep exercises short. However, students are expected to know which special journal is used to make the journal entry and how this will appear in the eight-column financial statements via the ledger account.

Exercises

7.1 As at 1 June 2009 a wholesaler in roof tiles has the following data (in €):

List of inventories

	Quantity	Price per sq m	Amount
Fast tiles:	220 sq m	9.50	2,090
Dutch tiles:	80 sq m	24.50	1,960
Cross tiles:	110 sq m	32	3,520
			7,570

List of accounts receivable

Bouwbedrijf Jansen	1,490
Het Nieuwe Huis	2,560
Bouwonderneming Versteeg	1,375
	5,405

List of accounts payable

Hollandse Betonfabriek	2,375
NV Dakpannen	3,390
	5,765

In June 2009 the following financial facts arose:

02/06   Received from Dakpannen JSC invoice I-37 for the delivery of:
200 sq m Dutch tiles   4,900
60 sq m cross tiles   1,920
                                                          6,820

The tiles have been stored today.

05/06   Sent invoice V-48 for the delivery of:
60 sq m Dutch tiles   1,920
70 sq m fast tiles   875
                                                          2,795

Invoice and tiles have been sent today to Bouwonderneming Versteeg.

08/06   Received invoice I-38 for the following tiles delivered by Hollandse Betonfabriek:
150 sq m fast tiles   1,425

09/06   Received cash statement B-33 referring to Het Nieuwe Huis LLC   1,120

10/06   Delivered to Het Nieuwe Huis LLC:
70 sq m fast tiles   875
60 sq m cross tiles   1,920
                                                          2,795

Both tiles and invoice V-49 have been sent today.

13/06	Paid cash (B-34) to:		
	Hollandse Betonfabriek	2,375	
	Dakpannen JSC	1,780	
			4,155
14/06	Received invoice I-39 from 'De Horizon' newspaper for advertising		750
15/06	Received from Het Nieuwe Huis 10 sq m fast tiles, returned because of wrong colour Credit invoice V-50 has been sent.		125
18/06	Sent invoice V-51 to Bouwbedrijf Jansen for tiles delivered today:		
	110 sq m Dutch tiles		3,520
19/06	Received credit invoice I-40 from Hollandse Betonfabriek referring to the 10 sq m fast tiles returned on 15/06		95
20/06	Received cash statement B-35:		
	Paid by Bouwbedrijf Jansen	1,490	
	Paid to 'De Horizon' newspaper 750		
	minus cash discount 15 –		
		735 –	
	Our cash account at the bank has been credited with		755
23/06	Sent invoice V-52 to Bouwonderneming Versteeg for delivering:		
	50 sq m cross tiles	2,100	
	60 sq m Dutch tiles	1,920	
			4,020
27/06	Received invoice I-41 from Dakpannen JSC for tiles received today:		
	100 sq m Dutch tiles	2,450	
	100 sq m cross tiles	3,200	
			5,650
29/06	Cash statement B-36 indicates:		
	Received from Bouwbedrijf Jansen	3,520	
	Bouwonderneming Versteeg	4,170	
		7,690	
	Paid to Dakpannen JSC	8,430	
	Cash account at bank debited with		740
30/06	Broken tiles written off(D-11):		
	4 sq m fast tiles	38	
	2 sq m Dutch tiles	49	
			87

Answer sheet **7.1 a** Using the above data, prepare the following sub-ledgers:
- accounts payable sub-ledger
- accounts receivable sub-ledger
- inventories sub-ledger.

7.1 b Prepare the balances of the following sub-ledgers as at 30 June:
- inventories sub-ledger
- accounts receivable sub-ledger
- accounts payable sub-ledger.

Answer sheet **7.2 a** Using the data in exercise 5.2, prepare the accounts receivable, accounts payable and inventories sub-ledgers.

b Check the balances in the sub-ledgers against the balances in the 'accounts receivable', 'accounts payable' and 'inventories' ledger accounts in exercises 5.2 or 6.2.

7.3 A grain wholesaler lists the following financial facts in September. Using the scheme shown, indicate what needs to be recorded in which special journal and/or sub-ledgers.

01/09 Purchased products on account for €1,000.

Solution:

Figure 7.27

Date	Special journals	Sub–ledgers
01/09	Purchase book	Accounts payable sub-ledger Inventories sub-ledger

02/09 Sold products on account for €2,500. Cost of goods sold €1,800. Products and invoice have been sent today.

05/09 Purchased products for €800, paid cash.

07/09 Received cash from a customer, €1,950.

08/09 Paid cash for various office expenses, €100.

11/09 Sold products for €500 cash. Products were purchased for €350.

12/09 Received invoice for filing cabinets purchased for €1,750. Cabinets and invoice received together.

15/09 Sold products for €3,000. Cost of goods sold €2,400. Half of the selling price is paid in cash; the other half will be paid in two months.

17/09   Purchased products on account for €1,700.

21/09   Paid the invoice for the filing cabinets in cash.

23/09   Purchased two desk chairs for €900, paid cash.

25/09   Paid cash to a supplier, €1,500.

27/09   Part of some goods with a purchase price of €200 have been returned. Credit invoice for €270 has been sent today.

29/09   Paid wages in cash, €700.

30/09   Depreciation of equipment for September is €200.

Answer sheet **7.4**   On 1 July 2009 Hoogeweg Company draws up the following lists (in €):

Inventories sub-ledger:
Televisions	20 pieces at 1,200	24,000
Stereo equipment	22 pieces at 800	17,600
Washing machines	25 pieces at 500	12,500
		54,100

Accounts receivable sub-ledger:
Borne Company, Amsterdam	12,816.20
Puts Company, Den Haag	8,251.50
	21,067.70

Accounts payable sub-ledger:
Niessen Company, Groningen	6,396.90
Schunke Company, Zwolle	9,977
	16,373.90

In July 2009, the following financial facts occurred, among others:

05 July   Purchased and received from Schunke Company, Zwolle, 6 washing machines (I-27)   3,000

07 July   Sold and delivered to Borne Company, Amsterdam, 10 televisions (V-43)   14,990

10 July   Sold and delivered to Puts Company, Den Haag, 5 washing machines (V-44)   3,495

11 July   Purchased and received from Schunke Company, Zwolle, 25 televisions (I-28)   30,000

12 July   Purchased and received from Niessen Company, Groningen, 15 pieces of stereo equipment (I-29)   12,000

14 July   Paid cash to Schunke Company, B-12   13,517

15 July	Returned to Niessen Company, Groningen, 3 pieces of stereo equipment due to some small damage (I-30)	2,400
17 July	Sold and delivered to Jansen Company, Utrecht, 12 pieces of stereo equipment	11,988
18 July	Sold and delivered to Puts Company, Den Haag, 6 washing machines (V-46)	4,194
20 July	Sent credit invoice (V-4) to Borne Company, discount due to small damage to a television	75
22 July	Received cash from Puts Company (B-13) for payment of 2 invoices, in total 12,375.60 minus 1% cash discount	12,251.84
25 July	Sold and delivered to Borne Company, Amsterdam, 3 pieces of stereo equipment (V-48)	2,997
28 July	Received invoice (I-31) from Schoonmaakbedrijf Stoffel for cleaning the building in July	400
29 July	Received cash statement B-14: Paid by Vorne Company 12,816.20 Paid to Biessen Company 6,396.90 –	6,419.30
30 July	Sold to H. Verschuur: a Mercedes, 3 years old. This is a company car with a book value of 16,000 (V-49)	14,000

Hoogeweg Company records the eventual credit invoices in the purchase or sales journal.

Using the above data, prepare and close, if necessary, the following journals: purchase journal, sales journal, accounts receivable sub-ledger, accounts payable sub-ledger and inventories sub-ledger.

Prepare journal entries in the purchase journal and sales journal.

Special entries

Having gained familiarity with the accounting process, there are still further frequent entries requiring our attention. Most enterprises have to deal with VAT (value-added tax) and some entrepreneurs may wish to obtain other data from the accounting system. These and certain other topics will be discussed in this part, using clear examples.

8 The decimal accounting system
9 VAT (value-added tax)
10 Withdrawals
11 Sales revenues
12 Various entries in cash books
13 Adjusting entries

The decimal accounting system

Part I demonstrated that the ledger is the heart of the accounting system since all financial facts in a firm are recorded here. At the end of the accounting period, a new balance sheet is prepared from the ledger and the income statement will show how equity has changed. So far, ledger accounts have been used in random order. In practice, similar ledger accounts are grouped together and numbered in a logical order. This has two main advantages:
1 In cash book and journal entries, only the number of the ledger account needs to be mentioned without the name of the account. Available space may be used to add an additional description or remark.
2 The number helps to identify the type of ledger account. By applying a certain account number classification it is possible to identify a balance sheet account or a specialised equity account, as well as to which category the ledger account belongs.

Decimal accounting system

Categories

- In classifying the ledger accounts we use the decimal accounting system. This implies classifying the ledger accounts in 10 categories, numbered 0 to 9.
- This is the most commonly used system of classification. In this course, the following six categories will be discussed. The following table gives an overview of ledger accounts and their category, together with an example.

Number	Account	Example
0	Fixed assets	Buildings, equipment
	Equity	Equity
	Long-term debt	Mortgage
1	Liquid assets	Cash
	Short-term receivables	Accounts receivable
	Short-term debt	Accounts payable, bank loans
4	Expenses	Energy costs, rent
7	Inventories	
8	Calculating sales profit	Gross profit
9	Incidental results	Profit/loss on selling fixed assets

Subgroups

Within the above categories, subgroups can be used, if required.
A second number is attached to the first number; the second number is that of the ledger account.
For example, the 'accounts receivable' ledger account. This is in category 1. The ledger account itself is numbered 2, so the ledger account number will be 1.2:
1.2 Accounts receivable

If we want to split accounts receivable by region, a number per region will be added.
1.2.1 Accounts receivable Groningen region
1.2.2 Accounts receivable Friesland region
etc.

It is even possible, within region, to classify reliability of debtors.
1.2.1.1 Accounts receivable Groningen region
1.2.1.2 Doubtful accounts receivable Groningen region
1.2.2.1 Accounts receivable Friesland region
1.2.2.2 Doubtful accounts receivable Friesland region
etc.

So it is clear that the numbering is fixed but that categorisation can be done as needed. Dots between numbers are usually removed.
If ledger accounts are classified in the right category, for preparation of the eight-column financial statements the numbers will show whether an account is an asset account, a liability account or a specialised equity account.
Asset and debt accounts can be found in categories 0, 1 and 7, specialised equity accounts in categories 4, 8 and 9. This knowledge also helps in preparing the eight-column financial statements.
The above numbering will be applied in the following chapters in this book.

Exercises

8.1 Give numbers to all the ledger accounts used in exercise 5.2. Each number should contain the number of the category and a follow-up number, so two numbers in total. Put the numbers in the right order.

VAT (value-added tax)

What does VAT mean?
Each enterprise is obliged to charge VAT on the amount received from customers for supplying goods and services. The customer may claim the VAT paid to the supplier from the tax authorities. The products will then be sold with a profit margin. The customer, now the supplier, charges VAT, to be paid to the tax authorities, on the new, higher price. So, ultimately, the entrepreneur pays VAT on the profit made, the 'value added'. Since the entrepreneur receives the VAT payable from the customer, and he pays the VAT receivable to the supplier, VAT does not affect the firm's profit at all; the entrepreneur is merely a transfer point. People who cannot claim VAT from the tax authorities (the final consumers) pay the full amount of VAT.
The VAT amount needs to be mentioned separately on all invoices.

■ **Example 9.1**

A bicycle retailer purchases a racing bike from his supplier for €800.
The purchase invoice looks as follows (in €):

Supplied: 1 racing bike	800
VAT 19%	152
	952

This bike will be sold for €1,000. The sales invoice is as follows (in €):

Delivered: 1 racing bike	1,000
VAT 19%	190
	1,190

The liability to the supplier includes €152 VAT. However, since this amount can be claimed, there will be a receivable of €152 from the tax authorities.
The receivable from the customer includes €190 VAT. At the same time there will be a liability to the tax authorities of €190.
On balance, €38 needs to be paid to the tax authorities, which equals 19% of the profit (= value added) of €200. ■

Not only VAT on purchases can be claimed, but also all VAT on expenses paid in cash, for instance an advance energy bill. However, the VAT amount needs to be mentioned on the cash document. There are three different tax rates: 19%, 6% (for example for food) and 0% (for international trade).
VAT will lead to adjustments in special journals and sub-ledgers.

The invoice needs to be recorded in the purchase journal, the accounts payable sub-ledger and the inventories sub-ledger. The columns in the special journals and sub-ledgers stay the same, apart from the purchase journal, in which a 'VAT' column will be added.

Figure 9.1

Purchase journal (in €)

Date	No.	Creditor	Total	VAT	ex VAT	Other	Account
		Supplier	952	152	800		

The full amount due is recorded in the 'supplier' account in the accounts payable book since this amount needs to be paid to the 'supplier':

Accounts payable book (in €)

Figure 9.2

Name 'Supplier'

Date	Accounting document	Debit	Credit	Balance
	Invoice		952	

The increase in the inventory will be recorded in the sub ledger inventories on the account 'racing bikes' excluding VAT. VAT does not increase the value of the inventories, it is a separate receivable.

Inventories sub-ledger (in €)

Figure 9.3

Name	Racing bikes				
Date	No.	Received from/Delivered to	Received	Delivered	Inventory
		Supplier	800		800

At the end of the accounting period, the following journal entry is made in the purchase journal, if no other invoices have been received (in €):

7		Inventories	800	
1		VAT receivable	152	
	1	Accounts payable		952

The entries made in the ledger, via the journal entry, in the 'inventories' and 'accounts payable' accounts, are exactly the same as the entries in the matching sub-ledgers.

The entries in the sales journal are similar to the previous entries (in €).

Figure 9.4

Date	No.	Debtor	Total	Sales revenue	VAT	Cost of goods sold	Other	Account
		Customer	1,190	1,000	190	800		

Figure 9.5

Name	'Customer'			
Date	Accounting document	Debit	Credit	Balance
	Invoice	1,190		1,190

Figure 9.6

Name	Racing bikes				
Date	No.	Received from/Delivered to	Received	Delivered	Inventory
		Supplier	800		800
		Customer		800	0

The journal entry of the sales journal is as follows (in €):

1		Accounts receivable	1,190	
	7	Inventories		800
	1	VAT payable		190
	8	Gross profit		200

Here also, after preparing the ledger the 'accounts receivable' and 'inventories' accounts match the sub-ledgers.

Remarks
- A credit invoice is a correction of a transaction already done. Here also, (negative) VAT needs to be calculated. The ledger account in which the VAT amount needs to be recorded is the same one as used for the initial transaction: for example, VAT on a credit invoice sent to the customer is (negative) VAT payable.

Recording VAT in the cash book speaks for itself. Chapter 6 has already shown how to split an amount received or paid.

Example 9.2

A cash slip showed the following (in €):

Stationery	200
VAT 19%	38
Paid cash	238

The VAT that has been paid in cash can be claimed from the tax authorities, so it does not influence expenses.
The 'cash' ledger account needs to be credited with €238 (accounting rule 3, see chapter 2). On the credit side of the cash book, the amount needs to be split into two amounts: after closing the cash book, the 'office expenses' ledger account needs to be debited with €200 (accounting rule 6) and the 'VAT receivable' ledger account with €38 (accounting rule 1).
We assume that the cash balance is €500.

Figure 9.7

Debit				Cash book (in €)				Credit
Date	No.	Account	Amount	Date	No.	Account	Amount
	Balance	500				Office expenses	200
						VAT receivable	38

Here also, the date and number of the accounting document do not have to be repeated.

If there will not be any other entries in the cash book, the journal entry will be (in €):

	4	Office expenses	200	
	1	VAT receivable	38	
		1 Cash		238

Remarks
- To record VAT, two ledger accounts are always used: VAT receivable and VAT payable. They are needed for filing the VAT form. Each period (month, quarter) a firm needs to report the sales revenue and the amount of VAT charged in that period, with the relevant tax percentage. VAT receivable is listed separately, of course related to the same period. The balance of VAT payable and VAT receivable is often recorded in a separate account: 'VAT paid'.
- Chapter 12 will discuss how VAT payable and VAT receivable are balanced.

Exercises

9.1 H.J. van Amersfoort started his business on 1 January 2009. He buys sacks of flour from two millers and sells these to bread factories. The flour is delivered in three different qualities: coarse-, medium fine- and fine-milled, and is packed in 25 kg sacks. Purchase and sales invoices are always received/sent with the sacks.

The following specialised equity accounts will be used:
Gross profit
Advertising expenses
Maintenance expenses
Rent
Interest expenses
Depreciation expenses
Various operating expenses
Various revenues and expenses

On 1 October 2009 the firm has the following data (in €):

Cash	461.75
Bank loan	1,720

List of accounts receivable:

'De Stad' bakery	6,573
Hooversma JSC	8,117
Menderson JSC	5,768
	20,458

List of accounts payable:

Miller R. van Slochteren	7,118
Foundation 'De Molen'	4,827
	11,945

List of inventories:

750 sacks coarse at 14	10,500
875 sacks of medium fine at 16	14,000
610 sacks of fine at 18	10,980
	35,480

During October the following financial facts occurred:

02/10	Received from Miller R. van Slochteren invoice I-37:	
	175 sacks coarse at 14	2,450
	100 sacks fine at 18	1,800
		4,250
	VAT 6%	255
		4,505

03/10	Received cash statement B-54:			
	Plus: 'De Stad' bakery	2,937		
	Menderson JSC	2,248		
		5,185		
	Minus: Miller R. van Slochteren	2,963		
	Foundation 'De Molen'	2,254		
		5,217 –		
	The bank has debited our account		32	
03/10	Sent invoice V-69 to Menderson JSC:			
	75 sacks coarse at 20	1,500		
	25 sacks medium fine at 22	550		
		2,050		
	VAT 6%	123		
			2,173	
04/10	Paid cash (K-45) for cleaning of office windows	60		
	VAT 19%	11.40		
			71.40	
09/10	Sent invoice V-70 to 'De Stad' bakery:			
	110 sacks coarse at 20	2,200		
	75 sacks fine	1,800		
		4,000		
	VAT 6%	240		
			4,240	
10/10	Received cash statement B-55:			
	Plus: Hooversma JSC	3,520		
	The bank has credited our account		3,520	
10/10	Received invoice I-38 from Foundation 'De Molen':			
	50 sacks coarse at 14	700		
	30 sacks medium fine at 16	480		
	40 sacks fine at 18	720		
		1,900		
	VAT 6%	114		
			2,014	
11/10	Paid cash for advertising expenses (K-46)	150		
	VAT 19%	28.50		
			178.50	
15/10	Sent invoice V-71 to Hooversma JSC:			
	150 sacks coarse at 20	3,000		
	120 sacks medium fine at 22	2,640		
	40 sacks fine at 24	960		
		6,600		
	VAT 6%	396		
			6,996	

16/10	Received cash statement B-56:		
	Plus: Menderson JSC	3,520	
	Minus: redemption of loan	5,000	
	interest last six months	3,200	
		8,200	
	The bank has debited our account		4,680
18/10	Sold to the local bakery, cash received (K-47):		
	25 bales fine at 24	600	
	VAT 6%	36	
			636
18/10	Received bank statement B-57:		
	Plus: 'De Stad' bakery	3,636	
	Minus: Miller R.van Slochteren	4,155 –	
	The bank has debited our account		519
19/10	Received invoice I-39 from Miller R. van Slochteren:		
	40 sacks coarse at 14	560	
	115 sacks medium fine at 16	1,840	
	25 sacks fine at 18	450	
		2,850	
	VAT 6%	171	
			3,021
21/10	Sent credit invoice VC-6 to Hooversma JSC because sacks damaged:		
	15 sacks coarse at 20	300	
	VAT 6%	18	
			318
21/10	Paid cash for repacking of the damaged sacks (K-48)	50	
	VAT 19%	9.50	
			59.50
22/10	Sent invoice V-72 to 'De Stad' bakery:		
	50 sacks coarse at 20	1,000	
	75 sacks medium fine at 22	1,650	
		2,650	
	VAT 6%	159	
			2,809
22/10	1 sack coarse damaged while loading the truck. It is unfit for sale. Accounting document D-14.		
25/10	Received invoice I-40 from Foundation 'De Molen':		
	70 sacks medium fine at 16	1,120	
	60 sacks fine at 18	1,080	
		2,200	
	VAT 6%	132	
			2,332

25/10	Received bank statement B-58:			
	Plus: Hooversma JSC	4,597		
	Menderson JSC	2,173		
		6,770		
	Minus: Miller R. van Slochteren	3,445		
	The bank has credited our account		3,445	
28/10	Sent invoice V-73 to Menderson JSC:			
	50 sacks medium fine at 22	1,100		
	150 sacks fine at 24	3,600		
		4,700		
	VAT 6%	282		
			4,982	
28/10	Paid cash (K-49) to Clean Company			
	for office cleaning	200		
	VAT 19%	38		
			238	
31/10	Received bank statement B-59:			
	Minus: Foundation 'De Molen'	2,573		
	Rent warehouse and office for October	700		
	The bank has debited our account		3,273	
31/10	Depreciation of equipment October (D-15)		180	

Answer sheet **9.2 a** Using the data given before, prepare: purchase journal, sales journal, cash book, special journal, and accounts receivable, accounts payable and inventories sub-ledgers. If necessary, close the journals and subledgers.

b Prepare journal entries from the special journals and mention the numbers of the ledger accounts used.

Answer sheet **c** On the basis of the journal entries, prepare and close the 'accounts receivable', 'accounts payable' and 'inventories' ledger accounts.

d Prepare lists of accounts receivable, accounts payable and inventories on the basis of the sub-ledgers.

e Check the totals of these lists with the ledger account balances.

Withdrawals

Private use

Withdrawing cash or products

The owner of a sole proprietorship may regularly withdraw cash or take products from the company for his or her own private use. It is also possible that the owner invests cash in the company, for example when cash is short.
Withdrawing cash or products can be regarded as the firm's 'redemption' of part of the 'liability' to the owner.
Payment into the firm increases the 'liability' to the owner of the firm.
Chapter 2 already showed that entries in the 'equity' ledger account are never made directly, which is why a new specialised equity account is introduced, the 'withdrawals' account, in category 0.

■ **Example 10.1**

Cash withdrawn for housekeeping €300.

The following will be recorded in the cash book (in €):

Figure 10.1

Debit				Cash book				Credit
Date	No.	Account	Amount	Date	No.	Account	Amount
		Balance	500			Withdrawal	300

The journal entry will be (in €):

0	Withdrawals		300	
	1	Cash		300

Chapter 9 showed that each firm needs to calculate VAT on goods and services it delivers. When the owner of a sole proprietorship takes products from the company, this is regarded as a delivery to the owner by the firm. VAT must thus be calculated and paid.

Example 10.2

Taken from the warehouse: products with a value of €160. VAT 19%.

This will be recorded in the general journal. VAT needs to be mentioned here to ensure the right journal entry is made.

Figure 10.2

General journal (in €)

Date	No.	Description	Amount
		Taken from warehouse for private use VAT 19%	160 30.40 190.40

Apart from this, an entry needs to be made in the inventories sub-ledger. The journal entry from the general journal is as follows (in €):

0		Withdrawals	190.40	
	7	Inventories		160
	1	VAT payable		30.40

Chapter 9 also showed that firms can claim VAT paid, but final consumers cannot. When a firm pays an amount that includes VAT which will be fully or partly charged to the owner, then the relevant part of the VAT cannot be claimed.

Example 10.3 (in €)

Invoice for gas, electricity and water	600
VAT 19%	114
Paid cash	714

One third of these expenses relates to the family home.

The amounts (in €) will be split:

	Firm	Private
Energy costs	400	200
VAT	76	38
	476	238

Only the firm's part of VAT can be claimed; the amount of €238, including VAT, will be recorded on the withdrawals account.

Figure 10.3

Debit				Cash book (in €)				Credit
Date	No.	Account	Amount	Date	No.	Account	Amount
		Balance	900			Energy costs	400
						VAT receivable	76
						Withdrawal	238

The journal entry is as follows (in €):

4	Energy costs	400	
1	VAT receivable	76	
0	Withdrawals	238	
	1 Cash		714

The 'withdrawals' ledger account is a specalised equity account, but its character is totally different from other specialised equity accounts. This is clear when one looks at the category in which the 'withdrawals' account appears, namely 0. The specialised equity accounts, assembled in the income statement in the eight-column financial statements, show the firm's profit or loss in the accounting year. The 'withdrawals' account, however, has nothing to do with the firm's profit or loss. That is why it is not desirable to show the balance of this account in the income statement. When preparing the eight-column financial statements, new equity will be calculated after preparing the income statement and before preparing the final balance sheet.

New equity will be calculated as follows:

Equity according to the 'balances' column   €
+ or – withdrawals according to the 'balances' column   €
(+ in case of credit balance, – in case of debit balance)
+ or – balance of income statement   €
(+ in case of profit, – in case of loss)
Equity in final balance sheet   €

Example 10.4

The following 'balances' are shown (in €):

Figure 10.4

Accounts	Balances		Income statement		Final balance sheet	
	Debit	Credit	Debit	Credit	Debit	Credit
Assets	100,000					
Debt		50,000				
Equity		30,000				
Withdrawals	5,000					
Gross profit		40,000				
Expenses	15,000					
Profit						
	120,000	120,000				

First, the specialised equity accounts (apart from the 'withdrawals' account) are assembled in the income statement, and profit or loss is determined (see chapter 3).

Figure 10.5 (in €)

Accounts	Balances		Income statement		Final balance sheet	
	Debit	Credit	Debit	Credit	Debit	Credit
Assets	100,000					
Debt		50,000				
Equity		30,000				
Withdrawals	5,000					
Gross profit		40,000		40,000		
Expenses	15,000		15,000			
Profit			25,000			
	120,000	120,000	40,000	40,000		

Afterwards, new equity is calculated (in €):

Equity according to 'balances'	30,000
Minus: debit balance 'withdrawals'	5,000
	25,000
Plus: profit	25,000
New equity	50,000

This amount will be recorded on the final balance sheet, together with the other asset and debt accounts (see chapter 3). ■

Figure 10.6 (in €)

Accounts	Balances		Income statement		Final balance sheet	
	Debit	Credit	Debit	Credit	Debit	Credit
Assets	100,000				100,000	
Debt		50,000				50,000
Equity		30,000				50,000
Withdrawals	5,000					
Gross profit		40,000		40,000		
Expenses	15,000		15,000			
Profit			25,000			
	120,000	120,000	40,000	40,000	100,000	100,000

In closing the 'withdrawals' ledger account the description is not 'balance' (since this account is not shown on the balance sheet), but 'equity' (closing the other ledger accounts has been discussed in chapter 4). The ledger account derived from the examples in this chapter looks as follows:

Figure 10.7

Debit			Withdrawals (in €)			Credit
Date	Description	Amount	Date	Description		Amount
	Cash book	300		Equity		728.40
	General journal	190.40				
	Cash book	238				
		728.40				728.40

Exercises

10.1 Mr. L. Spaander has problems in separating his private affairs from business matters. In relation to this, the following financial facts occurred in June 2009 (in €):

04/06	Took cash for housekeeping	400
07/06	Paid interim income tax statement via the firm's cash account	2,700
15/06	Taken from private cash account and transferred to the firm's cash	1,000
17/06	Paid maintenance expenses with private cash, including 19% VAT	71.40
18/06	Paid the energy bill via the firm's cash account, including €76 VAT. Three quarters of this amount relates to the firm	476
21/06	Paid a supplier from private cash account	1,350
25/06	Collected from warehouse products for private use, VAT included	309.40
28/06	Paid in cash an invoice for repair of door of family home, including 19% VAT	95.20

Prepare the journal entries the firm needs to make.
Add category numbers and, for each entry, which special journal and, if applicable, which special ledger needs to be updated.

Answer sheet **10.2 a** Finish the following eight-column financial statements. As description you can just write down the category number.

b Prepare the final balance sheet in scronto form. The debit side needs to be ranked by decreasing liquidity and the credit side by decreasing claimability.

Figure 10.8

Balances (in €)

Accounts		Debit	Credit
10	Buildings	250,000	
20	Equipment	70,000	
30	Mortgage		135,000
100	Bank loan		30,000
101	Cash	700	
180	VAT receivable	17,325	
181	VAT payable		35,813
0	Equity		115,785
1	Withdrawals		10,320
800	Gross profit		120,000
420	Depreciation expenses	21,000	
40	Loan	20,000	
430	Interest expenses	15,317	
910	Interest revenues		1,872
411	Energy expenses	5,790	
490	Various operating expenses	2,188	
110	Accounts receivable	37,441	
120	Accounts payable		53,284
410	Office expenses	2,533	
900	Various revenues and expenses		1,200
700	Inventories	60,980	
	Profit/loss	503,274	503,274

Sales revenues

We have been referring to the term 'gross profit'. It is not clear, however, to what sales revenue this gross profit relates. There might be a gross profit of €20,000. If there is sales revenue of €100,000, this result is good. But it will be different when the sales revenue is €1,000,000. Gross profit equals revenue minus purchase price. When the 'gross profit' specialised equity account is split into two specialised equity accounts, 'sales revenue' and 'cost of goods sold', then not only gross profit can be calculated by deducting cost of goods sold from sales revenue, but also total sales revenue.
See the example in chapter 9.

■ Example 11.1

A bicycle retailer purchases a racing bike from his supplier for €800.
The invoice looks as follows (in €):

Supplied: 1 racing bike   800
VAT 19%   152
                           952

This bike is sold for €1,000. The following invoice has been sent:

Delivered: 1 racing bike   1,000
VAT 19%   190
                           1,190

The following will be recorded in the sales journal (in €):

Figure 11.1

Sales journal

Date	No.	Account receivable	Total	Sales revenue	VAT	Cost of goods sold	Other	Account
		Debtor	1,190	1,000	190	800		

If we split gross profit, the following journal entry will be shown (in €):

1	Accounts receivable	1,190	
8	Cost of goods sold	800	
8	Sales revenue		1,000
7	Inventories		800
1	VAT payable		190

This journal entry can also be shown in two separate journal entries:

1	Accounts receivable	1,190	
8	Sales revenue		1,000
1	VAT payable		190

+

8	Cost of goods sold	800	
8	Inventories		800

Sometimes small enterprises do not keep a record of their inventories. This means that it will be hard to determine the cost of goods sold per sales transaction, particularly with changing purchase prices. Even if the cost of goods sold can be determined, small entrepreneurs do not bother to work out the related cost per transaction.

In this case only the first part of the journal entry needs to be recorded, both for cash sales and for sales on account.

The cost of goods sold will be recorded once per year, at the end of the accounting period, by stock taking (counting the inventories in the firm).

Example 11.2

A firm has the following data (in €):

Inventory 1 January	18,570
Purchases during the year (excluding VAT)	252,970
Sales during the year (excluding VAT)	294,640
Inventory 31 December	20,620

Cost of goods sold is calculated as follows:

Inventory 1 January	18,570
Plus: purchases	252,970
	271,540
Minus: inventory 31 December	20,920
Cost of goods sold	250,620

This amount can also be derived from the 'inventories' ledger account (in €):

Figure 11.2

Debit			Inventories			Credit
Date	Description	Amount	Date	Description		Amount
01/01	Balance	18,570	31/12	Sales journal		?
31/12	Purchase journal	252,970	31/12	Balance		20,920
		271,540				271,540

Since debit needs to equal credit, the missing number needs to be €250,620. In the income statement the 'sales revenue' account is shown on the credit side at €294,640 and the 'cost of goods sold' account on the debit side at €250,620. Gross profit is then €44,020.

Remarks
- When nothing is mentioned in the exercises, always use the 'sales revenue' and 'cost of goods sold' ledger accounts and split the full journal entry into two.

Exercises

11.1 Prepare journal entries for the following special journals. Use the 'sales revenue' and 'cost of goods sold' ledger accounts.
Indicate whether VAT is VAT receivable or VAT payable.
Note the category for all accounts used.

Debit side cash book (in €):

Sales revenue	10,600
VAT	2,014
Accounts receivable	78,553
Loan	10,000
Withdrawals	5,000

Credit side cash book (in €):

Car expenses	1,340
Office expenses	231
Maintenance expenses	192
VAT	335
Withdrawals	500
Accounts payable	89,517
Rent	750
Wages	1,500
Energy costs	1,115
VAT	143

Purchase journal (in €):

'Total' column	379,610
'VAT' column	60,610
'Inventories' column	311,500
'Various' column:	
• General expenses	2,000
• Auditing costs	5,500

Sales journal (in €):

'Total' column	400,792
'Sales revenue' column	336,800
'VAT' column	63,992
'Cost of goods sold' column	293,700

Credit purchase journal (in €):

'Total' column	18,326
'VAT' column	2,926
'Inventories' column	15,400

Credit sales journal (in €)
'Total' column	9,758
'Sales revenue' column	8,200
'VAT' column	1,558
'Cost of goods sold' column	6,760

General journal (in €)
Taken from warehouse for own use, including 19% VAT	238
Depreciation of equipment	170
Cost of goods sold for cash	9,150

11.2
1	Cash sales	10,234
2	Cash purchases	9,996
3	Sales on account	100,674
4	Purchases on account	81,872
5	Credit invoices sent	2,618
6	Credit invoices received	2,856
7	Inventory 1 January	17,850
	Inventory 31 December	16,320

a Prepare journal entries for the above data, indicating the category.

b Calculate gross profit.

Various entries in cash books

Some financial facts have not yet been discussed. Examples will be used to examine these.

Example 12.1

VAT

Clearing of VAT in the third quarter of the year (in €):
- VAT payable   27,800
- VAT receivable   15,400
- Paid cash   12,400

After this payment, the VAT liability reduces by €27,800; the 'accounts payable' ledger account needs to be debited (accounting rule 4, see chapter 2). At the same time the VAT receivable is reduced; the 'accounts receivable' ledger account needs to be credited (accounting rule 3).
This can be realised by a cash payment of €12,400, the balance of a payment of €27,800 and a receipt of €15,400.

Figure 12.1

Debit				Cash book (in €)				Credit
Date	No.	Account	Amount	Date	No.	Account	Amount	
		Balance VAT receivable	5,000 15,400			VAT payable	27,800	

The following entries are made (in €):

	1	Cash		15,400	
		1	VAT receivable		15,400
	1	VAT payable		27,800	
		1	Cash		27,800

Wages

■ **Example 12.2**

Gross wages September		2,500
Withheld: wages tax	800	
social contributions	300	
		1,100
Paid cash		1,400
Employer's part of social contributions		500

Wages tax and social insurance premiums – social contributions – need to be paid to the tax authorities (like the 'transfer point' system for VAT in chapter 9). On top of these amounts, paid by the employee, the employer needs to pay part of the insurance premiums. This is known as the employer's part of social contributions.

The €1,100 cash payment can be split into a payment of €2,500 and receipts of respectively €800 and €300. These receipts immediately form a debt to the tax authorities and to the trade union.

Figure 12.2

Debit				Cash book (in €)				Credit
Date	No.	Account	Amount	Date	No.	Account		Amount
		Balance	2,000			Wages		2,500
		Wages tax and social contributions payable	1,100					

The following journal entries result (in €):

	1	Cash		1,100	
		1	Wages tax and social contributions payable		1,100
and:					
	4	Wages		2,500	
		1	Cash		2,500

The employer's part of social contributions is an extra amount to be paid to the trade union. This results in expenses, but also in a liability.
The employer's part will be recorded in the general journal.

Figure 12.3

General journal (in €)

Date	No.	Description	Amount
		Employer's part of social security contributions September	500

The journal entry is as follows (in €):

4	Social contributions		500	
	1	Wages tax and social contributions payable		500

The 'social contributions' ledger account is a specialised equity account. Social contributions withheld from gross wages are not an expense: the firm is again the 'transfer point'.

Remarks
- Several alternatives exist for recording VAT payment as well as wages and wage payments. Transitory accounts in the ledger are most often used in this case.
- Wages are usually recorded in a special specialised journal. This will not be explored in this introductory course. Finally, the same records will be made in the ledger.

Example 12.3

Paid by a customer	€	10,000
Minus: 2% discount for cash payment	€	200
Cash received	€	9,800

With the payment of €9,800, the total receivable of €10,000 disappears. This means that the 'accounts receivable' ledger account needs to be credited for €10,000.
Here also, the receipt of €9,800 must be split into a receipt of €10,000 and a payment (expenses) of €200.
We create a specialised equity account: 'discounts'.

Figure 12.4

Debit				**Cash book** (in €)				Credit
Date	No.	Account	Amount	Date	No.	Account	Amount
		Balance	5,000			Discounts	200
		Accounts receivable	10,000				

The following journal entries result (in €):

1	Cash		10,000	
	1	Accounts receivable		10,000
and:				
4	Discounts		200	
	1	Cash		200

Pay attention
In the accounts receivable sub-ledger, the account of the relevant debtor needs to be credited with €10,000, since this amount will be recorded in the 'accounts receivable' ledger account via the journal entry (see chapter 7 too).

Apart from the above examples, other problems with accounting documents may occur. However, they can all be solved in the way described here.

Exercises

12.1 A firm has the following cash receipt documents in November 2009 (in €).

01/11	Cash balance			737
02/11	K-84: Paid office expenses	150		
	VAT 19%	28.50		
				178.50
04/11	K-86: Paid to supplier	1,800		
	Cash discount	36 –		
				1,764
11/11	K-88: Paid for advertising in local newspaper	370		
	VAT 19%	70.30		
				440.30
15/11	K-89: Cleared with Kabola JSC:			
	Their receivables	2,640		
	Our receivables	1,780 –		
	Paid			860
18/11	K-90: Cash sales	820		
	VAT 19%	155.80		
				975.80
19/11	K-91: Paid for outside cleaning of building	120		
	VAT 19%	22.80		
				142.80
22/11	K-92: Received from customer			600
	Agreed that total receivable of 750 has been cleared.			
27/11	K-94: Paid to tax authorities:			
	withheld wage tax and social contributions October	790		
	Employer's part social contributions	120		
				910
29/11	K-95: Paid to tax authorities:			
	VAT payable	1,950		
	VAT receivable	830 –		
				1,120

30/11	K-96: Gross wages		1,800	
	Withheld wage tax	520		
	Social contributions	270		
			790 −	
	Paid			1,010

Answer sheet **12.2 a** Prepare and close the cash book for November 2009.

b Make the journal entry, indicating the categories of the ledger accounts.

c Indicate which entries need to be made in a sub-ledger. Indicate the relevant sub-ledger, the amount, and whether the amount needs to be debited or credited.

Adjusting entries

At the end of the accounting year, after closing, the whole accounting process needs to be checked. This check is done after the balances have been prepared, but, obviously, before preparing the income statement and the final balance sheet. Possible mistakes can still be corrected and forgotten entries can still be included.
These corrections are entered in the general journal and from here journal entries will be made. The balances will be corrected afterwards with the amounts shown in the journal entries. This will be shown in some examples.

The following balances are given (in €):

Figure 13.1

Balances

Accounts		Debit	Credit
010	Equipment	42,000	
000	Equity		127,530
001	Withdrawal	7,620	
700	Inventories	57,970	
180	VAT receivable	2,710	
181	VAT payable		10,850
800	Cost of goods sold	396,270	
801	Sales revenue		432,190
100	Cash	31,570	
110	Accounts receivable	55,910	
120	Accounts payable		47,220
400	Housing costs	10,840	
410	Office expenses	7,960	
420	Various expenses	4,940	
		617,790	617,790

Example 13.1

Products taken from the warehouse for private use with a value of €200, excluding 19% VAT. This has not been recorded yet.

This results in the following journal entry (in €):

001	Withdrawals		238	
	181	VAT payable		38
	700	Inventories		200

Example 13.2

Paid cash for housing costs €184 excluding VAT. By accident, the costs are recorded at €148. VAT has been recorded correctly.

First, the wrong entry is analysed by looking at the journal entry made of this transaction (in €):

400	Housing costs		148	
	100	Cash		148

This entry needs to be cancelled by making an opposite entry:

100	Cash		148	
	400	Housing costs		148

Then the right journal entry needs to be made:

400	Housing costs		184	
	100	Cash		184

The two correcting journal entries can be joined in the following journal entry:

400	Housing costs (184 – 148)		36	
	100	Cash		36

Example 13.3

A purchase invoice for equipment of €1,904 including VAT has been accidentally recorded in 'inventories'.
First we look at the wrong entry:

700	Inventories		1,600	
180	VAT receivable		304	
	120	Accounts payable		1,904

The opposite journal entry will be made:

120	Accounts payable		1,904	
	700	Inventories		1,600
	180	VAT		304

13 Adjusting entries

The correct entry is:

010	Equipment		1,600	
180	VAT receivable		304	
	120	Accounts payable		1,904

In this way all the wrong entries can be corrected.

Finally, the balances are adjusted by including the data from the three journal entries.

Figure 13.2

Balances (in €)

Accounts		Debit	Credit
010	Equipment	43,600	
000	Equity		127,530
001	Withdrawal	7,858	
700	Inventories	56,170	
180	VAT receivable	2,710	
181	VAT payable		10,888
800	Cost of goods sold	396,270	
801	Sales revenue		432,190
100	Cash	31,534	
110	Accounts receivable	55,910	
120	Accounts payable		47,220
400	Housing costs	10,876	
410	Office expenses	7,960	
420	Various expenses	4,940	
		617,828	617,828

After preparing the adjusted balances, the income statement and the final balance sheet can be prepared in the usual way.

Exercises

13.1 When checking the accounts at year-end, the following issues were revealed:

1. A cash payment for advertising costs of €300, excluding 19% VAT, has accidentally been recorded in the 'energy costs' account.

2. The last cash statement from the bank has not yet been recorded. Received from debtor Velema €2,099.16. This refers to invoice V-148, €2,142, including 19% VAT. A 2% cash discount for payment within 14 days has been deducted.

3. A cash payment of €5,290 to creditor Dierks has accidentally been recorded in the cash book for €5,920. The entry in the accounts payable sub-ledger is correct.

4. A cash sale of trade-in products has been recorded as sale of new products. Data: selling price €1,785, including 19% VAT, cost of goods sold €1,100. Sales revenue and cost of goods sold are recorded separately for new products; however, for trade-in products only gross profit is recorded.

5. The sale of a company car for €14,280, including 19% VAT, has been recorded on the 'company cars' ledger account for the full amount (excluding VAT). At the moment of sale the car's book value was €13,500.

Referring to the above data, prepare the adjusting entries. Indicate categories.
Also indicate possible corrections in a sub-ledger, and what sort of correction.

13.2 An electrical equipment firm has the following balances as at 31 December:

Figure 13.3

Balances (in €)

Accounts		Debit	Credit
010	Equipment	68,761	
000	Equity		112,792
001	Withdrawal	7,927	
800	Sales revenue, household equipment		277,915
810	Cost of goods sold, household equipment	242,513	
801	Sales revenue, industrial equipment		408,334
811	Cost of goods sold, industrial equipment	361,852	
820	Gross profit, second-hand equipment		19,128
180	VAT receivable	15,912	
181	VAT payable		27,644
400	Maintenance expenses	17,883	
120	Accounts receivable	42,636	
130	Accounts payable		39,284
100	Cash	16,772	
410	Wages	26,900	
420	Depreciation expenses	3,115	
490	Office expenses	29,826	
700	Inventory, household equipment	22,973	
701	Inventory, industrial equipment	26,313	
710	Inventory, second-hand equipment	1,714	
		885,097	885,097

After checking the accounts, the following mistakes were identified:

1 A cash bill for office expenses, €476, including 19% VAT, has not been recorded yet.

2 Maintenance expenses, €500 excluding VAT, has accidentally been recorded in the 'wages' acccount.

3 A sale of household equipment has been recorded as a sale of second-hand equipment. Invoice data (in €):

   Sales revenue   800
   VAT 19%   152
                   952

   Cost of goods sold 700.

4 A credit invoice received for industrial equipment, €1,904 including 19% VAT, has been recorded as a normal purchase invoice.

a Prepare the adjusting entries.

Answer sheet   b Prepare the adjusted balances.

Answer sheet   c Prepare income statement and final balance sheet.

International aspects of accounting

In the first two parts of this book you learned the basics of financial accounting. In the final parts you will learn how to use the outcomes of the accounting process.
The final goal of the subject financial accounting is to provide information for management to make decisions and to evaluate performance.
In the coming three chapters you will learn what formats can be used for accounting, how to measure financial performance based on ratio analysis and the function of a cash flow statement.

14 Various formats of financial statements
15 Ratio analysis
16 Cash flow statements

Various formats of financial statements

Chapter 1 explained the need for financial information.
Generally speaking, the objective of financial statements is to provide and facilitate information for the decision-making process and assess the accountability of managers.
Financial statements are the most effective way to inform insiders and outsiders about the economic performance of a given company on a periodic basis.
You have learned how the accounting process works, how financial data are structured in the 'double entry book-keeping system'.
The end result is a balance sheet and an income statement.

Classified balance sheet:

The balance sheets shown in the previous chapters were divided into three parts: 'Assets, Liabilities and Owner's Equity'. You can imagine that even small companies will have 'hundreds' of accounts listed in these categories and this will not help you much to analyse the performance of a given company.

Classified balance

A classified balance sheet shows the sub-categories and filters the accounts; in doing so, it provides a comprehensive overview.

Duffy's Place, a local café in Utrecht, had the following balance sheet (in €):

Figure 14.1

Debit	Balance sheet 31 December 2006		Credit
Equipment	22,000	Equity	64,380
Furniture, restaurant	36,000	Bank loan	45,000
Building	44,500	Accounts payable	8,900
Inventory	16,235	VAT payable	7,755
Accounts receivable	3,600		
Cash	3,700		
Total	126,035	Total	126,035

As outlined in Part I, the balance sheet represents the financial position of a company at a particular point in time.

The following sub-categories are used here:
Current Assets: inventory, accounts receivable and cash
Fixed Assets: property, plant and equipment
Current Liabilities: accounts payable, short-term loans, other payables
Long-term Liabilities: long-term loans, bonds
Owners' Equity.

The way in which sub-categories are presented depends mainly on the location from which one is operating. First shown here is the 'European Model'. If we insert the sub-categories, the classified balance sheet will look like this:

Figure 14.2 — Balance sheet 31 December 2006

Assets			Liabilities and Owners' Equity (in €)		
		31 Dec 2006			31 Dec 2006
Fixed Assets			Owners' Equity		
Building	44,500		Paid in capital	60,000	
Furniture, restaurant	36,000		Retained earnings	4,380	
Equipment	22,000				64,380
		102,500	Long-term Debt		
Current Assets			Bank loan		45,000
Inventory	16,235				
Accounts receivable	3,600		Current Liabilities		
Cash	3,700		Accounts payable	8,900	
		23,535	VAT payable	7,755	
					16,655
Total Assets		126,035	Total Liabilities and Owners' Equity		126,035

If the company operates in North America, the balance sheet will look as follows:

Figure 14.3

Balance sheet

Assets			Liabilities and Owners' Equity (in €)		
		31 Dec 2006			31 Dec 2006
Current Assets			Current Liabilities		
Cash	3,700		VAT payable	7,755	
Accounts receivable	3,600		Accounts payable	8,900	
Inventory	16,235				16,655
		23,535	Long-term Debt		
Fixed Assets			Bank loan		45,000
Equipment	22,000		Owners' Equity		
Furniture, restaurant	36,000		Paid in capital	60,000	
Building	44,500		Retained earnings	4,380	
		102,500			64,380
Total Assets		126,035	Total Liabilities and Owners' Equity		126,035

The numbers, the accounts and the sub-categories are the same, though the way the accounts are 'ranked' is different.

A closer look at the different sub-categories:

Assets:

Current Assets:
Current Assets are cash or other assets that are expected either to be converted into cash, to be sold or to be consumed within one year.

For Duffy's Place this basically means that the products they have in stock (such as beverages) will be sold to customers and will finally, after a certain period of time, lead to a cash inflow for the company. Depending on the type of inventory, this operating flow can last just a few days, such as in the case of perishable goods, e.g. fresh milk, or it can take a few months, as with consumer goods, e.g. expensive whisky.
For accounts receivable this means that the sale has already been made, but the cash inflow will be realised in a following accounting period.

Fixed Assets:
The Fixed Assets category includes those long-term assets used in the continuing operation of the company. They are necessary in the production of the goods and services for customers.
The café needs chairs, tables and bar stools to accommodate their customers, for which the total investment can be found in the Furniture, restaurant account. Depreciation and the cost/expense of these assets can be spread over a period of several years. The prefix 'fixed' is not the only definition of the Fixed Assets category; other definitions are also used for this classification, e.g. tangible assets, operating assets or plant assets.

Liabilities:

Current Liabilities:
Current Liabilities consist of obligations that must be paid within a year. These liabilities are normally paid with cash 'that flows in' from current assets or from new short-term loans. In our example, this is cash to be paid to suppliers (accounts payable) and to the government in the form of taxes e.g. VAT. There are further types of current liabilities, such as short-term debt, wages payable, customers who prepay and similar.

Long-Term Liabilities:
Long-term liabilities or long-term debts (LTD) are debts that mature more than one year in the future. Bank loans, mortgage payable and employee pension obligations generally fall in this category.

Owners' Equity
Owners' equity is the account representing the value invested by the owners in the company. When the owners of a small business starts their business, their savings are invested in the business. Over the years, this amount can increase, because part of the after-tax net profit is kept in the company. Please note that the owners of a small business who are also responsible for the day to day running of the company must be rewarded economically on two fronts:
- their invested money
- direct income from labour

The owners/entrepreneurs have no fixed salary, and so can only obtain money for personal use (e.g. buying food or schoolbooks for their kids) by making withdrawals from the company's accounts.

The following overview illustrates the flow (in €):

Owners' equity on 31 Dec 2006:	64,380
Net profit after taxes 2007:	+ 31,388
Owners' equity without withdrawals =	95,768
Private withdrawals in 2007	– 26,000
Owners' equity on 31 Dec 2007	69,768

The owners' equity increased in 2007 by €5,388 (€31,388 – €26,000). In many companies a special account, retained earnings, is used to record this amount.

Classified income statement:
A *classified income statement* gives the overview of revenues and expenses for a specific period of time. If we take Duffy's Place as an example, the income statements from recent years are as follows (in €):

Figure 14.4

Income statements	2006		2007		2008
Sales		225,000		232,000		222,000
Cost of sales	67,500		74,240		74,800	
Gross profit		157,500		157,760		147,200
Wages	51,750		51,040		47,650	
Maintenance costs	13,500		14,000		14,500	
Other costs	32,750		31,900		31,680	
Depreciation	9,500		9,500		9,500	
Total operating expenses		107,500		106,440		103,330
Earnings Before Interest and Taxes (EBIT)		50,000		51,320		43,870
Interest expenses	6,600		6,480		6,230	
Net income before taxes		43,400		44,840		37,640
Taxes 30%	13,020		13,452		11,292	
Net income after taxes		30,380		31,388		26,348
Private withdrawals		26,000		26,000		26,000
Increase in equity		4,380		5,388		348

The income statement provides information about a company's economic performance in a specific period, based on historical data. For management purposes, it is expedient, even for small businesses, to be able to produce an income statement more than once a year. Based on the results for the period, management can then assess the situation and decide what action, if any, should be taken.

Before we take the next step, that of evaluating performance, we first need to take a closer look at some pertinent items.

1 Gross profit

Gross profit expresses how much a company earns on its sales. This is the difference between the sales price and the purchase price. For instance, if demand is down and the company reacts by lowering its prices, but the company is not able to buy the goods from its suppliers at a lower rate, then gross profit will fall. Whether this leads to a final net profit that is lower will ultimately depend on how other expenses can be managed and/or, in this case, reduced.

Here we can calculate the gross profit ratio for 3 years:

Figure 14.5

	2006	2007	2008
Gross profit/sales	70%	68%	66%

The margin remains under pressure during this period.

2 EBIT

This abbreviation stands for: Earnings Before Interest and Taxes.
It expresses the economic performance of the 'day to day business' activity. In this case business activity is offering 'entertainment' and selling drinks and snacks. It is also called Operating Income or Profit Before Interest and Taxes.
If you look at the development of EBIT over the 3-year period, you will see that the EBIT performance deteriorated over 2008.

3 Net income after taxes

The net income after taxes 'belongs' to the owners, as compensation for the hours spent working in the company and for capital invested. In order to measure whether or not the capital invested by the owners was beneficial, we need to take into account labour costs for a managing director.

The labour costs in this case are (in €):

2006: 28,000
2007: 29,000
2008: 29,500

Compensation for the invested capital/equity is:

Figure 14.6 (in €)

	2006	2007	2008
Net income after taxes	30,380	31,388	26,348
Compensation for labour	28,000	29,000	29,500
Compensation for Owners' Equity	2,380	2,388	(3,152)

In other words, the capital invested by the owners showed a positive return in 2006 and 2007, but a negative one in 2008. These returns should be compared with alternative investments that carry the same level of risk. Although the 2008 results were negative, this does not mean that this was a really bad result, unless it can be compared with the same type of investment in the same market, over the same period of time.

Exercises

14.1 Make a classified balance sheet and income statement based on exercise 13.2

14.2 The following accounts are provided for Heineken, the huge Dutch international brewing company, based on the adjusted annual report of 2009 (in €):

Figure 14.7

Revenues	14,319
Income tax expenses	248
Investments in associates	1,257
Interest expenses	485
Trade and other receivables	2,904
Depreciation	1,236
Capital	710
Retained earnings	?
Personnel expenses	2,425
Bank overdrafts	94
Trade and other payables	3,846
Tax liabilities	119
Property and plant	5,950
Raw materials and services	9,578
Cost of goods sold	?
Loans and borrowings	9,084
Cash and cash equivalents	698
Operating profit	1,080
Inventories	1,470
Profit before income taxes	?
Equipment	864
Net profit after taxes	347

Questions
1. What is the cost of goods sold in 2009?
2. How much was the profit before income taxes in 2009?
3. What is the amount of retained earnings in the balance sheet?
4. Make a classified balance sheet for Heineken.
5. Make a classified income statement.

15 Ratio analysis

As mentioned before, book-keeping is not a goal in itself. It was not invented to create jobs for book-keepers or accountants. It is just a means to obtain relevant information for the managers and stakeholders of the company. This information can be evaluated by ratio analysis. In ratio analysis one compares the performance of the business from two perspectives:
1. How has performance developed over the years (horizontal analysis)?
2. How does the performance of the company compare with its competitors, the benchmark (vertical analysis).

The concept of comparisons is crucial, since this identifies trends in the business and allows action to be taken.
A ratio is a kind of shorthand for a business's financial position or operations expressed in a number. Its first purpose is to identify areas that need further investigation. It gives an indication only, not the story behind the numbers. The numbers should always be combined with inside information on relevant issues. The ratio analysis should be used with a good general understanding of the company, its environment and developments in the market, including competition.

The financial statements (balance sheet and income statement) of Duffy's Place for the last three years:

Balance sheets (in €)

Figure 15.1

Assets				Liabilities and Owners' Equity			
Balance sheet	31 Dec 2006	31 Dec 2007	31 Dec 2008		31 Dec 2006	31 Dec 2007	31 Dec 2008
Current Assets				**Current Liabilities**			
Cash and equivalents	3,700	2,049	10	Taxes (VAT)	7,755	8,896	7,983
Accounts receivable	3,600	2,800	7,600	Accounts payable	8,900	9,450	21,456
Inventory	16,235	18,765	21,445		16,655	18,346	29,439
	23,535	23,614	29,055	**Long-term Debt**			
Fixed Assets				Bank loan	45,000	37,500	34,000
Equipment	22,000	29,000	39,000	**Owners' Equity**			
Furniture, restaurant	36,000	33,000	30,000	Paid in capital	60,000	60,000	60,000
Building	44,500	40,000	35,500	Retained earnings	4,380	9,768	10,116
	102,500	102,000	104,500		64,380	69,768	70,116
				Total Liab+Owners' Equity			
Total Assets	126,035	121,555	133,555		126,035	125,614	133,555

Income statements

Figure 15.2

Income statements		2006		2007		2008
Sales		225,000		232,000		222,000
Cost of sales	67,500		74,240		74,800	
Gross Profit		157,500		157,760		147,200
Labour costs	51,750		51,040		47,650	
Building operating costs	13,500		14,000		14,500	
Other costs	32,750		31,900		31,680	
Depreciation	9,500		9,500		9,500	
Total operating expenses		107,500		106,440		103,330
EBIT		50,000		51,320		43,870
Interest expenses	6,600		6,480		6,230	
Net income before taxes		43,400		44,840		37,640
Taxes 30%	13,020		13,452		11,292	
Net income after taxes		30,380		31,388		26,348
Private withdrawals		26,000		26,000		26,000
Increase in Equity		4,380		5,388		348

Liquidity

Liquidity means whether the company is able to pay its short-term invoices on time. To answer this question you need to know how much should be paid in the short run (current liabilities), and what kind of sources are available in cash, or in accounts that will lead to cash, in the short run (current assets).

In the ratio analyses we start with two ratios, current ratio and quick ratio (in €):

Figure 15.3

		2006	2007	2008
Current ratio:	Current assets/	23,535	23,614	29,055
	Current liabilities	16,655	18,346	29,439
		1.41	1.29	0.99

Figure 15.4

		2006	2007	2008
Quick ratio:	Current assets minus Inventories/	7,300	4,849	7,610
	Current liabilities	16,655	18,346	29,439
		0.44	0.26	0.26

If the benchmark for the current ratio is 2.0 and for the quick ratio 0.5, what does it tell you about the liquidity of this company? Be aware of the fact that companies can be 'creative' with these ratios when they want to demonstrate good liquidity. For instance, by postponing necessary investments in fixed assets they can show a good cash position in the short run, but it is just 'window dressing' for the liquidity position.

Working capital

Working capital is a financial metric that represents operating liquidity in a business. Along with fixed assets such as plant and equipment, working capital is considered a part of operating capital. It is calculated as current assets minus current liabilities. If current assets are less than current liabilities, an entity has a working capital deficiency, also called a working capital deficit.

Net working capital (in €)

Figure 15.5

		2006	2007	2008
NWC	Current assets	23,535	23,614	29,055
	Current liabilities	16,655	18,346	29,439
	Net working capital	6,880	5,268	384 negative

Other ratios linked with liquidity include:

Inventory turnover

Inventory turnover is the number of times the inventory is sold.

Formula:

Cost of goods sold/Average inventory

Figure 15.6 (in €)

		2007	2008
Cost of goods sold / Average inventory 2008:	(16,235 + 18,765) / 2 (18,765 + 21,445) / 2	74,240 17,500	74,800 20,105
		4.2	3.7

It turned out that it takes longer to sell the average inventory.

Average days to sell inventory

Average days to sell inventory indicates how long it takes, on average, to sell your inventory.

Formula:

Days in a year/Inventory turnover

Figure 15.7

	2007	2008
Days/ Inventory turnover	365 4.2 86 days	365 3.7 98 days

If the inventory turnover decreases, then the ratio for the average days to sell the inventory should go up, because the inventory turnover is the denominator in the formula. In this case we already concluded that it takes more time to sell the average inventory: based on the calculation, you can see that it took on average 12 days more to sell the average inventory, not a good development. The company has to take measures to reduce the level of inventory, while considering the needs of their customers.

Receivable turnover

Receivable turnover shows the number of times receivables are collected.

Formula:

Sales/Average accounts receivable

Figure 15.8 (in €)

	2007	2008
Sales/	232,000	222,000
Average accounts receivable 2007: (3,600 + 2,800) / 2 2008: (2,800 + 7,600) / 2	3,200	5,200
	73	43

Average collection period

Average collection period measures how long it takes for customers to pay their invoices.

Formula:

$$\text{Average accounts receivable/Sales} \times 365 \text{ days}$$

Figure 15.9

	2007	2008
Days	365	365
Receivable turnover	73	43
	5 days	9 days

Here you can see the same, a trend that we have seen for the inventory: it takes longer to achieve the cash inflows. Please take into account that, for this type of company (cafés), customers pay directly after they have ordered. As can be seen, this is not a huge amount compared with the other accounts on the balance sheet, although the customers still need to pay their bill! What is shown by the two ratios can be seen on the balance sheet too: the amount of receivables increased sharply in 2008.

- Average is calculated by: (beginning position – ending position) / 2

Profitability

Profitability measures the relationship between investments and return (= profit).
A company's profitability is linked to its liquidity because we may assume that profits will, in the long term, lead to cash inflows. However, be aware that profit is not necessarily equal to the cash balance: not all expenses are cash outflows (e.g. depreciation).

Four relevant ratios:

Profit margin

Profit margin measures net profit in relation to sales.
The profit margin that we use is the profit before tax. For comparing companies in an industry we focus on the operating performance and want to eliminate the effect of different taxes in different countries.

$$\text{Formula: Net profit (before taxes)/ Sales} \times 100\%$$

Figure 15.10

	2007	2008
Net profit (before taxes)	44,840	37,640
Sales	232,000	222,000
	19.3%	17.0%

If the benchmark gives an average in 2008 of 16%, then the company scored well compared with its competitors.

Asset turnover

Asset turnover measures how efficiently assets are used to generate sales.

Formula:

Sales/Average of total assets

Figure 15.11 (in €)

	2007	2008
Sales	232,000	222,000
Average of total assets	125,825	129,585
Turnover:	1.84	1.71

2007: (126,035 + 125,614) / 2
2008: (125,614 + 133,555) / 2

The ratio decreased due to the fact that sales dropped more than the total investment.

Return on assets

Return on assets (ROA) measures the productivity of the total capital (debt and equity).

Formula:

$$ROA = \text{Net profit} + \text{interest}/\text{Average total assets} \times 100\%.$$

Figure 15.12 (in €)

	2007	2008
Net profit (before taxes)	44,840	37,640
Interest	6,480	6,230
Average of total assets	125,824.5	129,585
ROA	40.8%	29.5%

For every € that is invested in this company there was a return of 40.8% in 2007 and of 29.5% in 2008. That is a respectable return.

Return on equity

Return on equity (ROE) measures the profitability for the owners/shareholders.

Please take into account that we use the 'full amount' of net profit before taxes but we do not include the amount calculated for the owner's labour! The reason is that most companies have a legal structure whereby the owner is also an employee. So, in this case, their salary is part of the total labour expenses reflected in the income statement.

Formula:

$$\text{Net profit/Average owners' equity} \times 100\%$$

Figure 15.13 (in €)

	2007	2008
Net profit	44,840	37,640
Average owners' equity	67,074	69,942
ROE	67%	54%
2007: € (64,380 + 69,768) / 2		
2008: € (69,768 + 70,116) / 2		

The returns are rather high, but that is not exceptional for small businesses, which are more labour intensive than capital intensive.

Solvency

Solvency is the ability to survive in the long term. Solvency ratios indicate whether or not a company is 'on the road to bankruptcy'. If a company makes a loss, equity will decrease by the amount of the loss. The more a company is financed with equity the more it is able to cover losses and continue inbusiness. In terms of solvency, it is relatively safe for debt holders when a company is financed with a relatively high amount of equity.

Two ratios measure the solvency of a company:

$$\text{Total liabilities/Owners' equity}$$

Figure 15.14 (in €)

	2006	2007	2008
Total liabilities (current liabilities + long-term debt)	61,655	55,846	63,439
Owners' equity	64,380	69,768	70,116
Ratio:	0.99	0.80	0.90

To give an indication, the debt-to equity ratio for banks is 11.5: in Lehman's it was 44 in the year they went bankrupt! There are no general rules about a good standard for this ratio; it depends on trust.

Please realise that the value of assets on the balance sheet is based on the assumption that business will be continued. When the company cannot continue, however, the market value of assets may be far lower than the value based on the accounting rules. The resulting deficit will decrease equity.

Interest coverage ratio

Interest coverage ratio:
The interest coverage ratio measures the degree of protection lenders have from a default in interest payment. The higher the number, the less risk there is for the lenders.

Formula:

$$(\text{Net profit before taxes} + \text{Interest expenses})/\text{Interest expenses}$$

Figure 15.15 (in €)

	2006	2007	2008
Net profit (before taxes) + interest	50,000	51,320	43,870
Interest expenses	6,600	6,480	6,230
Ratio:	7.6	7.9	7.0

Overview:

Figure 15.16

Ratio	2006	2007	2008	Comment
1 Current ratio	1.41	1.29	0.99	Not so good
2 Quick ratio	0.44	0.26	0.26	Not so good
3 Inventory turnover	n.a	4.2	3.7	Not good
4 Average days for inventory	n.a	86 days	98 days	Not good
5 Receivable turnover	n.a	73	43	Not so good but relatively unimportant
6 Average collection period	n.a	5 days	9 days	Not so good but relatively unimportant
7 Profit margin	n.a	19.3%	17.0%	Ok compared with the industry, but a negative tendency
8 Asset turnover	n.a	1.84	1.71	
9 Return on assets (ROA)	n.a	40.8%	29.5%	
10 Return on owners' equity (ROE)	n.a	67%	54%	Quite high but deteriorating
11 Debt-to-equity ratio	0.99	0.80	0.80	Not very risky
12 Interest coverage ratio	7.6	7.9	7.0	Not very risky

Exercises

15.1 Humphrey's Restaurants are a Dutch chain. The consolidated balance sheet and income statement for recent years were as follows (in €):

Humphrey's Restaurants 1,000							
Balance sheet				December 31:			
Fixed Assets	2009	2008	2007	Owners' Equity	2009	2008	2007
Property and plant	2,650	2,730	2,785	Capital	1,510	1,510	1,510
Equipment	2,734	2,698	2,734	Retained earnings	2,876	2,854	2,788
	5,384	5,428	5,519		4,386	4,364	4,298
Current Assets				**Non-current Liabilities**			
Inventories	2,555	2,456	2,365	Loans and borrowings	2,657	2,787	2,907
Trade and other receivables	1,571	1,413	1,399	**Current Liabilities**			
				Bank overdrafts	594	623	734
Cash and cash equivalents	712	655	456	Trade and other payables	2,466	1,898	1,555
	4,838	4,524	4,220	Tax liabilities	119	280	245
					3,179	2,801	2,534
	10,222	9,952	9,739		10,222	9,952	9,739

Income statement 1,000	2009	2008	2007
Revenues	12,556	12,789	12,112
Cost of goods sold	4,678	4,776	4,887
Gross Profit	7,878	8,013	7,225
Operating Expenses:			
Personnel expenses	3,466	3,455	3,378
Depreciation: property etc.	1,236	1,200	1,164
Depreciation: equipment	345	360	375
Other expenses	764	754	771
Operating Profit	2,067	2,244	1,537
Interest expenses	485	491	501
Profit before income taxes	1,582	1,753	1,036
Income tax expenses	443	491	290
Net Profit after taxes	1,139	1,262	746

		Industry average
1	Current ratio	2.0
2	Quick ratio	0.8
3	Net working capital	n.a
4	Inventory turnover	6.1
5	Average days of inventory	60
6	Receivable turnover	12
7	Average collection period	30
8	Profit margin	15%
9	Asset turnover	1.5
10	ROA	20%
11	ROE	28%
12	Debt-to-equity ratio	1.5
13	Interest coverage ratio	4

Questions

1 Calculate the ratios for Humphrey's for the accounting years 2008 and 2009.
2 What conclusions can you draw about Humphreys' performance if you consider the trend and in comparison with the industry average. Split your conclusions into three parts: Liquidity, Profitability and Solvency.

Cash flow statements

Duffy's Place made a profit over the last 3 years; the net profit after tax was greater than the cash needed for private use. The retained income account increased in 2006 and 2007.
However, the cash balance at the end of 2008 was only €10.
What happened in 2008? Is the company still able to pay its invoices on time?

The final topic in this book is the cash flow statement, which shows cash inflows and cash outflows within an accounting period, usually a year.

The classified cash flow statement has three categories:

Cash flows from operating activities

a Cash flows from operating activities focuses on the income statement and how the income statement relates to operating cash flows.

Cash flows from investing activities

b Cash flows from investing activities focuses on fixed assets and how investments and disinvestments influence cash flows.

Cash flow from financing activities

c Cash flow from financing activities focuses on long-term debt and equity, and how these sources of finance influence the cash flow.

Operating activities are those that reflect the daily activities of the company.
Examples of cash inflow: payments from customers; examples of cash outflows: payments for wages, payments for interest and tax, and to suppliers.

Investing activities are those that will affect the Fixed Assets accounts on the balance sheet.
Examples of cash outflow: purchase of property, plant and equipment; examples of cash inflow: sale of property, plant and equipment.

Financing activities are those that will affect Owners' Equity and Long-term Liabilities, Examples of cash outflow: repayments of loans; examples of cash inflow: borrowing from banks, cash investment by the owners.

The balance sheets of Duffy's Place at the beginning and at the end of 2008 looked as follows:

Figure 16.1   **Balance sheet**

Assets			Liabilities and Owners' Equity		
	31 Dec 2007	31 Dec 2008		31 Dec 2007	31 Dec 2008
Fixed Assets			**Owners' Equity**		
Building	40,000	35,500	Paid in capital	60,000	60,000
Furniture, restaurant	33,000	30,000	Retained earnings	9,768	10,116
Equipment	29,000	39,000		69,768	70,116
	102,000	104,500	**Long-term Debt**		
Current Assets			Bank loan	37,500	34,000
Inventory	18,765	21,445			
Accounts receivable	2,800	7,600	**Current Liabilities**		
Cash and equivalents	2,049	10	Accounts payable	9,450	21,456
	23,614	29,055	Taxes (VAT)	8,896	7,983
				18,346	29,439
Total Assets	125,614	133,555	**Total Eq and Liab**	125,614	133,555

At the beginning of the year the cash balance was €2,049, but at the end of the year only €10!

If you *compare* two balance sheets of one company in two periods, then, by definition, the *differences* on the left side equal the *differences* on the right side.
In this case the left side changed from €125,614 to €133,555 = €7,941, which equals the change on the right side of the balance sheet.

Figure 16.2   **Balance sheet**

Assets				Liabilities and Owners' Equity			
	31 Dec 2007	31 Dec 2008	Change		31 Dec 2007	31 Dec 2008	Change
Fixed Assets				**Owners' Equity**			
Building	40,000	35,500	4,500–	Paid in capital	60,000	60,000	
Furniture, restaurant	33,000	30,000	3,000–	Retained earnings	9,768	10,116	348
Equipment	29,000	39,000	10,000		69,768	70,116	
	102,000	104,500		**Long-term Debt**			
Current Assets				Bank loan	37,500	34,000	3,500
Inventory	18,765	21,445	2,680				
Accounts receivable	2,800	7,600	4,800	**Current Liabilities**			
Cash and equivalents	2,049	10		Accounts payable	9,450	21,456	12,006
	23,614	29,055		Taxes (VAT)	8,896	7,983	913
					18,346	29,439	
Total Assets	125,614	133,555		**Total Eq and Liab,**	125,614	133,555	
Total change			9,980	**Total change**			7,941
Cash etc.	2,049	10	2,039				

The total change on the left side of the balance sheet (Fixed Assets and Current Assets, except the cash account), increased by €9,980.

The total change on the right side of the balance sheet (Owners' Equity, Long-term Debt and Current Liabilities) increased by €7,941.

Without the cash account, the left side increased €2,039 (= € 9,980 – € 7,941) more than the right side, which matches the change in the cash account.

The effect of the changes in assets and liabilities/equity on the cash position is as follows:

If a specific asset account increases it has a *negative* affect on the cash position if payment is made in the same accounting period.
For instance, if a company invests in fixed assets, such as buying new equipment, then this has a negative effect on the cash account if paid for immediately.

If a specific asset account decreases it has a *positive* affect on the cash position in the relevant accounting period.
For instance, if the total amount of accounts receivable dropped, this cash would have flowed into the cash account! In the case of Duffy's Place we can see that two accounts on the debit side decreased: Fixed Assets were depreciated (reducing book value). Be aware that depreciation expense is *not* a cash flow.

If a specific account for liabilities/equity increases it has a *positive* effect on the cash account in the relevant accounting period.
For instance, accounts payable (cash to be paid to suppliers) went up by €12,006.
If the company had paid the invoices, they would have had less cash.

If a specific liabilities/equity account decreases it has a *negative* effect on the cash account within the relevant accounting period.
For instance, in Duffy's Place the total amount that has to be paid to the tax office decreased by €913. If they had not saved this 'extra' amount, then the cash balance would be €913 lower.

The following overview summarises the above (in €):

Figure 16.3

	Sources		Spending
Decrease building	4,500	Increase equipment	10,000
Decrease furniture, restaurant	3,000	Increase inventory	2,680
Increase retained earnings	348	Increase accounts receivable	4,800
Increase accounts payable	12,006	Decrease bank loan	3,500
		Decrease taxes	913
	19,854		21,893
Result: Decrease in cash	2,039–		

Additional information to illustrate what happens in cash flows:

a   At the end of December 2008 the company was offered a special Italian espresso machine and an ice-making machine for a total price of €12,000. Under normal market conditions the price of the two machines would have been at least €20,000. The owner accepted the offer and the machines were delivered at the end of December 2008.

The invoice was partly (€4,000) paid by borrowing extra money from the bank (long-term debt); the remainder (€8,000) still needs to be paid to the supplier, and forms part of accounts payable in the balance sheet of 31 Dec 2008.
The new machines will be depreciated from 2009 onwards.

b   The total depreciation for the fixed assets is €9,500:
  i   Equipment   € 2,000
  ii Furniture, restaurant € 3,000
  iii Building   € 4,500

c   The owner withdrew €26,000 from the cash account for private use.

The partial income statement for 2008 is as follows (in €):

Figure 16.4

	2008
Sales	**222,000**
Cost of sales	74,800
Gross Profit	**147,200**
Labour costs	47,650
Building costs (rent)	14,500
Other costs	31,680
Depreciation	9,500
Total operating expenses	103,330
Profit from operations	**43,870**
Interest expenses	6,230
Net income before tax	37,640
Taxes 30%	11,292
Net income after tax	**26,348**

Indirect method

There are two methods of preparing the cash flow statement: the direct and the indirect methods. Here we will discuss the *indirect method*, since the direct method is beyond the scope of this introductory book.

Before explaining this method, first consider the following question: Suppose you have to measure the cash flow of a market vendor who is buying and selling oranges.
He has no employees, he pays his suppliers in cash and the customers pay directly in cash when they buy the oranges.

All other expenses are paid directly.
There are no fixed assets, so no difficult depreciation calculations.
There is no inventory at the end of the day: oranges left over after a working day will be delivered to the homeless people's centre.
Question: Where do you start in order to measure the cash flows for this market vendor over one operating day?
Answer: His wallet!
Right. The cash flow is the difference between the cash position early in the morning before paying for the new stock, and late in the afternoon when the last sale is arranged.

Others may call it the net income!
That's true too, but only in this case
For this company Net Income = Net Cash Flow. There are no time lags between the moment the expense is taken onto the income statement and cash outflow, and the revenues that will lead to cash inflows.
There are no difficulties in measuring the relevant expenses and revenues for a certain period.
There are no fluctuations in inventories, or payables to suppliers.
There is no debt and no fixed assets, so life is simple.

To gain a clear picture of the cash flows for a certain period the indirect method is used.

Cash flow from operating activities

The indirect method calculates the *cash flow from operating activities*, as follows:

Net income
Add: Depreciation
        Decrease in accounts receivable
        Decrease in inventories
        Increase in accounts payable
        Increase in other payables
        Incidental losses
Deduct: Increase in accounts receivable
        Increase in inventories
        Decrease in accounts payable
        Decrease in other payables
        Incidental profits.

The 2008 cash flow from operating activities is as follows (in €):

Figure 16.5

	Indirect method	Cash inflow	Cash outflow	
	Operations			
1	Net income after taxes	26,348		
2	Add back: Depreciation	9,500		
3	Increase in inventory		2,680	
4	Increase in accounts receivable		4,800	
5	Increase in accounts payable	12,006		
6	Decrease in taxes payable		913	
	Net cash inflow from operations	**39,461**		

Investing activities

Cash flow from investing activities:

The fixed asset account shows:

+ Book value of fixed assets at beginning of year   €

+ Investments during the year   €

− Depreciation during the year (no cash flow!)   €

= Book value of fixed assets at end of year   €

Disinvestments and sales of fixed assets will have a negative value based on the book value.

In the case of Duffy's Place, there are three accounts in the fixed assets category:
  Building
  Furniture, restaurant
  Equipment

Based on the above structure, and the additional information on page 132 (investment of €12,000 in equipment) and the depreciation from the income statement, we can measure the relevant cash flow for investments.
  The total depreciation for 2008 was €9,500
  For the building account €4,500
  For the furniture, restaurant account €3,000
  For the equipment account €2,000

The related cash flow can be calculated as follows (in €):

Building:

+ Book value: building 31 Dec 2008   40,000

+ Investments during the year   –

− Depreciation during the year   4,500

= Book value: building 31 Dec 2008   35,500

Disinvestments and sales of fixed assets will have a negative value based on the book value.

Book values at the beginning and end of the year are derived from the balance sheets.

From the above it is clear that there has been no cash flow related to the building in 2008.

Furniture, restaurant:

+ Book value: furniture, restaurant 1 Jan 2008   33,000

+ Investments during the year   –

– Depreciation during the year   3,000

= Book value: furniture, restaurant 31 Dec 2008   30,000

So, here also, the cash flow is zero.

Equipment:

+ Book value: equipment 1 Jan 2008   33,000

+ Investments during the year   12,000

– Depreciation during the year   2,000

= Book value: equipment 31 Dec 2008   29,000

The cash flow from investing activities is €12,000.

Figure 16.6 (in €)

	Cash inflow	Cash outflow
Investment		
1 Buying new equipment		12,000
Cash flow from Investments		12,000

Financing activities

Cash flow from *financing activities:*

For cash flows from financing activities we have to focus on the cash inflow and outflow for long-term debt and owners' equity.

If a company borrows money, this results in a cash inflow; if the company reduces debt, it leads to a cash outflow.
In 2008 the company took out a new loan of €4,000.

In the case of equity, cash inflow is the money invested by the owner to finance the business.

The cash flow related to debt is calculated as follows (in €):

+ Value of long-term debt at 1 Jan 2008   37,500

+ Receipt of new loan in 2008 (cash inflow)   4,000

– Payback of loan in 2008 (cash outflow)   7,500

= Value of long-term debt at 31 Dec 2008   34,000

The value of the loan at the beginning and end of the year can be derived from the balance sheets, and should be in line with the conditions of the contract.

The above example showed that there was a cash inflow of €4,000 and a cash outflow of €7,500 in 2008.

The cash flow related to equity is calculated as follows:

+	Retained earnings at 1 Jan 2008	9,768
+	Net income after taxes 2008	26,348
–	Withdrawals for private use (cash outflow)	26,000
=	Retained earnings at 31 Dec 2008	10,116

So, the cash outflow for withdrawals was €226,000.

Figure 16.7 (in €)

	Cash inflow	Cash outflow
Financing		
1 Taking a new loan	4,000	
2 Paying back loan		7,500
3 Private withdrawals		26,000
Cash outflow from financing		**29,500**

Total overview of the cash flow statement (in €):

Figure 16.8 (in €)

Indirect method	Cash inflow	Cash outflow
Operations		
1 Net income after taxes	26,348	
2 Add back: Depreciation	9,500	
3 Increase inventory		2,680
4 Increase accounts receivable		4,800
5 Increase accounts payable	12,006	
6 Decrease taxes payable		913
Net cash inflow from operations	**39,461**	
Investments		
1 Buying new equipment		12,000
Cash flow from investments		**12,000**
Financing		
1 Taking a new loan	4,000	
2 Paying back loan		7,500
3 Private withdrawals		26,000
Cash outflow from financing		**29,500**

	Cash inflow	Cash outflow
Cash inflow from operations	39,461	
Cash flow from investments		12,000
Cash outflow from financing		29,500
Net cash outflow		2,039

The cash account decreased in 2008 by €2,039, which matches the cash balances at the beginning (€2,049) and end of the accounting year (€10).

The investment at the end of the year had a huge negative impact on the cash position of the business.

Exercises

16.1 The entertainment company Joy Forever wonders why they have been facing difficulties with their cash flows over the last year, although the company still made a reasonable profit.

The balance sheet and income statement are (in €):

Balance sheet	2009	2008	December 31: Owners' equity	2009	2008
Fixed Assets			**Owners' equity**		
Property and plant	160,000	165,000	Capital	50,000	50,000
Equipment	50,000	45,500	Retained earnings	40,000	37,000
				90,000	87,000
	210,000	210,500	**Non-current Liabilities**		
Current Assets			Loans and borrowings	140,000	130,000
Inventories	60,000	53,000	**Current Liabilities**		
Trade and other receivables	5,000	2,500	Bank overdrafts	13,000	12,000
Cash and cash equivalents	6,000	15,000	Trade and other payables	30,000	45,000
	71,000	70,500	Tax liabilities	8,000	7,000
				51,000	64,000
	281,000	281,000		281,000	281,000

Income statement	2009	2008
Revenues	300,000	310,000
Cost of goods sold	100,000	110,000
Gross Profit	200,000	200,000
Operating expenses:		
Personnel expenses	125,000	120,000
Depreciation: property etc,	5,000	5,000
Depreciation: equipment	7,000	6,000
Other expenses	15,000	14,000
Operating Profit	48,000	55,000
Interest expenses	14,000	13,000
Profit before income taxes	34,000	42,000
Income tax expenses 30%	10,200	12,600
Net Profit after taxes	23,800	29,400

Retained earnings 31 Dec 2008	37,000
Net Profit after taxes	23,800
Private withdrawals	20,800
Retained earnings 31 Dec 2009	40,000

Prepare the cash flow statement.

Case study: Hoovers

Having studied the first three parts of this course, students will have an adequate knowledge of accounting.
The case here in Part IV enables the student to show how financial facts in a small firm for a period of one month can be recorded. This finally results in a balance sheet and income statement, providing insight into the firm's financial position.

Case study: Hoovers

Mr. and Mrs. Hoovers run a wholesale business in wide-screen televisions. In the regions Groningen, Friesland, Drenthe and Overijssel they are sole traders for three brands, bought directly from the importers. The brands and importers are:

- from Japan: Sawaki JSC, importer, Amsterdam
- from America: Superset, importer Meroga LLC, Enschede
- from France: Valder, importer Manders, Groningen.

Products and invoices are received at the same time.

The wide-screen televisions are sold to three retail chains specialising in audiovisual equipment. These chains are:
- Beeld en Geluid JSC, 3 locations, headquarters in Assen
- Discount House LLC, 4 locations, office in Emmen
- Fantasia LLC, 4 locations, headquarters in Hoogeveen.

Products and invoices are sent to the chains' headquarters, which take care of further distribution themselves.
Previously the firm also supplied products to Rekkers LLC in Meppel, however, this company is in bankruptcy. Hoovers still has an outstanding receivable with this firm.

Hoovers' payment conditions mention 2% discount when payment is within 8 days; 30 days net.
Freight costs, €100, will be charged for orders under €5,000 (excluding VAT); orders above this amount are free from freight costs.
For transporting products, a van was bought 3 years ago for €28,000 (excluding VAT).

Hoovers employs one man, who takes care of the warehouse and distribution with the van.

For some time Mr. and Mrs. Hoovers have been looking for somebody to take over the firm since they are approaching retirement age. In June 2009 a candidate appeared. In order to set the price of the business, a balance sheet was prepared as at 1 July 2009.

This take-over, however, has not materialised. There is now a new candidate who wants to see a balance sheet as at 1 August 2009, the possible date for the take-over.

Data as at 1 July 2009 are as follows (in €):

Figure 17.1

Balance sheet 01 July 2009			
Van	11,200	Equity	42,996
Equipment	8,500	Loan	15,000
Inventory	27,850	Accounts payable	55,200
Accounts receivable	6,700	VAT payable	8,214
VAT receivable	5,929	Wages tax and social contributions payable	1,890
Cash	3,121		
	123,300		123,300

List of accounts receivable:
Beeld en Geluid JSC, Assen		invoice V-58	11,650	
		invoice V-59	11,550	
				23,200
Discount House LLC, Emmen		invoice V-57	9,600	
		Invoice V-60	12,650	
				22,250
Fantasia LLC, Hoogeveen		invoice V-61	13,650	
Rekkers LLC, Meppel		invoice V-37	7,600	
				66,700

List of accounts payable:
Leenders JSC, Amsterdam		invoice I-44	12,400	
		invoice I-48	12,950	
				25,350
Meroga LLC, Enschede		invoice I-45	10,200	
		Invoice I-47	11,050	
				21,250
Manders Company, Groningen		invoice I-46		8,600
				55,200

List of inventories:
Sawaki: 17 sets at 750	12,750	
Superset: 12 sets at 850	10,200	
Valder: 7 sets at 700	4,900	
		27,850

Hoovers uses the following ledger accounts:

000 Equity
001 Withdrawals
010 Van
020 Equipment
050 Van
100 Cash
110 Accounts receivable
120 Accounts payable
140 Wages tax and social contributions payable
160 VAT receivable
161 VAT payable
400 Rent
401 Office expenses
402 Energy costs
410 Wages
411 Social contributions
420 Car expenses
430 Depreciation expenses
440 Interest expenses
700 Inventory
800 Sales revenue
801 Cost of goods sold
910 Discounts received
920 Discounts given
990 Various revenues and expenses

During July 2009, the following financial facts occurred (in €):

01/07	Sent invoice V-62 to Beeld en Geluid JSC		
	4 Sawaki at 950	3,800	
	2 Superset at 1,100	2,200	
	2 Valder at 900	1,800	
		7,800	
	VAT 19%	1,482	
			9,282
02/07	Sent invoice V-63 to Discount House LLC		
	4 Sawaki at 950	3,800	
	2 Superset at 1,100	2,200	
		6,000	
	VAT 19%	1,140	
			7,140
03/07	Received invoice I-49 from Meroga LLC	10,200	
	VAT 19%	1,938	
			12,138

03/07	Received cash statement no. 81			
	plus: Fantasia LLC, invoice V-61	13,650		
	Cash discount	285 −		
			13,365	
	minus: Leenders JSC, invoice I-44	12,400		
	Manders, invoice I-46	8,600		
		21,000 −		
	The bank debited our account with		7,635	
06/07	Received credit-invoice I-50 from Meroga LLC			
	Quantity discount second quarter	400		
	VAT 19%	76		
			476	
07/07	Received bank statement no. 82:			
	plus: Beeld en Geluid JSC, invoice V-58	11,650		
	Discount House, invoice V-57	9,600		
			21,250	
	minus: Rent for warehouse, office, and family home, August (rent for family home is 650)	2,200 −		
	The bank has credited our account with		19,050	
07/07	Cash payment slip nr. 72:			
	Paid for petrol	36		
	VAT 19%	6.84		
			42.84	
09/07	Sent invoice V-64 to Fantasia LLC			
	4 Sawaki at 950	3,800		
	3 Superset at 1,100	3,300		
	5 Valder at 900	4,500		
		11,600		
	VAT 19%	2,204		
			13,804	
10/07	Received invoice I-51 from Leenders JSC			
	8 Sawaki at 750	6,000		
	VAT 19%	1,140		
			7,140	
10/07	Cash payment slip no. 74:			
	Paid for maintenance of van	284		
	VAT 19%	53.96		
			337.96	
10/07	Sent credit invoice V-65 to Discount House LLC for returned products:			
	2 Valder at 900	1,800		
	VAT 19%	342		
			2,142	

13/07	Received invoice I-52 from Wolters LLC			
	2 desk chairs at 400		800	
	VAT 19%		152	
				952

13/07 Received cash statement no. 83:
plus: Discount House LLC, invoice V-60   2,650
minus: Petty cash   1,500 –
The bank has credited our account with   12,150

13/07 Received credit invoice I-53 from Leenders JSC
for returned products:
2 Valder at 700   1,400
VAT 19%   266
                                                    1,666

15/07 Received cash statement no. 84:
plus: Rekkers LLC   750
(this is final payment of bankrupt firm;
the remaining receivable is uncollectable)

minus: Leenders JSC, invoice I-48   12,950
Meroga LLC, invoice I-45   10,200
Minus credit invoice I-50   476 –
                                          9,724
                                         22,674
The bank has debited our account with   21,924

15/07 Received invoice I-54 from Manders
8 Valder at 700   5,600
VAT 19%   1,064
                                                    6,664

16/07 Cash payment slip no. 75:
Paid for petrol   42
VAT 19%   7.98
                                                    49.98

17/07 Cash payment slip no. 76:
Sold a desk with chair for book value   120
VAT 19%   22.80
                                                   142.80

17/07 Sent invoice V-66 to Discount House LLC
2 Sawaki at 950   1,900
1 Superset at 1,100   1,100
1 Valder at 900   900
                                          3,900
Freight charges   100
                                          4,000
VAT 19%   760
                                                    4,760

17/07	Internal document D-15: Taken from the warehouse for private use			
	1 Valder		700	
	VAT 19%		133	
				833
20/07	Received cash statement no. 85:			
	plus: Beeld en Geluid, invoice V-59		11,550	
	minus: Paid wage tax and social contributions second quarter		1,890	
	Bank has credited our account with			9,660
21/07	Cash payment slip no. 77:			
	Paid for petrol		38	
	VAT 19%		7.22	
				45.22
22/07	Received cash statement no. 86:			
	plus: Fantasia LLC, partial payment invoice V-64		7,000	
	minus: Clearing VAT June			
	VAT payable	8,214		
	VAT receivable	5,929 –		
			2,285 –	
	Bank has credited our account with			4,715
23/07	Sent invoice V-67 to Fantasia LLC			
	6 Sawaki at 950		5,700	
	5 Superset at 1,100		5,500	
			11,200	
	VAT 19%		2,128	
				13,328
23/07	Received invoice I-55 from Leenders JSC			
	12 Sawaki at 750		9,000	
	VAT 19%		1,710	
				10,710
27/07	Received cash statement no. 87:			
	plus: Discount House LLC, Invoice V-63		7,140	
	minus: Credit invoice V-65		2,142	
			4,998	
	minus: Electricity bill		500	
	VAT		95	
			595	
	(one fifth needs to be charged to the family home)			

		Wolters LLC, invoice I-52	952	
		Meroga LLC, invoice I-47	11,050	
			12,597	
		The bank has debited our account with		7,599

27/07	Cash payment slip no. 78: Petty cash collected from bank		1,000

27/07	Received invoice I-56 from Wolters LLC		
	Various stationery	80	
	VAT 19%	15.20	
			95.20

28/07	Received invoice I-57 from Meroga LLC		
	5 Superset at 850	3,400	
	VAT 19%	646	
			4,046

28/07	Sent invoice V-68 to Beeld en Geluid JSC		
	2 Sawaki at 950	1,900	
	2 Superset at 1,100	2,200	
		4,100	
	Freight charges	100	
		4,200	
	VAT 19%	798	
			4,998

30/07	Received cash statement no. 88:		
	minus: Redemption of loan	2,500	
	Six-month interest	300	
	Petty cash	1,000	
	The bank has debited our account with		3,800

31/07	Cash payment slip no. 79:			
	Gross wages		1,500	
	Wages tax	375		
	Social contributions	45		
	Withheld		420	
	Paid			1,080

31/07	Internal document D-16:
	Employer's part social contributions is 14% of the gross wages.

31/07	Internal document D-17:
	Depreciation August:
	Van: 2% of purchase price
	Equipment: 5% of value as at 1 July.

On behalf of Mr. Hoovers, prepare the accounts for July, taking the following steps:

Answer sheet	**16.1**	Open the ledger, the cash book, and the sub-ledgers with the data as at 1 July. Indicate the name of the ledger accounts, and also the matching category number.
	16.2	Enter the financial data in the special journals and the sub-ledgers. Category numbers may be used as description in the special journals.
	16.3	Close the special journals.
	16.4	Prepare journal entries in the special journals, Here also, just use the category numbers.
	16.5	On the basis of the journal entries, prepare the ledger accounts. As description the special journal in which the journal entry was made should be used.
	16.6	Prepare the balances in the eight-column financial statements.
	16.7	Compare the balances in the cash book and the totals in the sub-ledgers with the related balances.
	16.8	Prepare the income statement and the final balance sheet.
	16.9	Prepare the final balance sheet in sconto form: the debit side ranked according to increasing liquidity and the credit side increasing claimability.
	16.10	Prepare the balance sheet showing the categories.
	16.11	Prepare a ratio analysis.
	16.12	Prepare the cash flow statement.

Index

accounts *17*
accounts payable *12*
accounts payable sub-ledger *63*
accounts receivable *12*
accounts receivable sub-ledger *58, 63*
asset turnover *124*
assets *12*
average collection period *123*
average days to sell inventory *122*

balance sheet *12*
balances *27*

cash flow from financing activities *129*
cash flows from investing activities *129*
cash flows from operating activities *129, 133*
categories *76*
classified balance *112*
classified income statement *115*
closing the accounts *33*

credit side *12*

decimal accounting system *76*

equity *12*

final balance sheet *29*
financing activities *135*

general journal *52*

income statement *28*
indirect method *132*
interest coverage ratio *126*
inventories sub-ledger *63*
inventory turnover *122*
investing activities *134*

journals *46*

ledger *17*
liabilities *12*
liquidity *121*

private use *88*
profit margin *123*
profitability *123*
purchase book *46*

ratio analysis *119*
receivable turnover *122*
return on assets *124*
return on equity *125*

sales book *46*
solvency *125*
specialised equity accounts *21*
subgroups *77*

trial balance *27*

VAT *100*

wages *101*
withdrawing cash or products *88*
working capital *121*

151